DOWN THE VILLAGE STREET

When Peter Douglas left a well-paid
industrial job in the Midlands and
came to run a village post office and
general stores in deepest Norfolk, he
and his wife were complete strangers
to country life and village ways.
What they found was so unexpected
and so hilarious that it had to be
written down . . .

'The stories he relates about the life
of the village will delight town and
country dwellers alike.'
Sunday Express

Peter Douglas

Down the Village Street

Illustrations by Martin Honeysett

CORGI BOOKS
A DIVISION OF TRANSWORLD PUBLISHERS LTD

DOWN THE VILLAGE STREET

A CORGI BOOK 0 552 11256 9

First published in Great Britain by The Boydell Press Ltd.

PRINTING HISTORY
Boydell Press edition published 1978
Corgi edition published 1980
Copyright © 1978 by P. W. Douglas

This book is set in Intertype Baskerville

Corgi Books are published by
Transworld Publishers Ltd,
Century House, 61–63 Uxbridge Road,
Ealing, London W5 5SA
Set, printed and bound in Great Britain by
Cox & Wyman Ltd, Reading

Author's note: *All characters in this book are imaginary, and bear no resemblance to living persons.*

CONTENTS

ONE

THE DECISION

IT was really Maggie who started the whole thing off. That was odd, because as the breadwinner I was supposed to be the one who made all the major decisions.

It had been building up for some time, of course, but Maggie was the one who had made her mind up, and then had done something about it. The three-legged cat was involved in the decision somewhere. He hadn't caused us to make up our minds, but he had somehow become a symbol to us, a symbol of all the things that we didn't want out of life. Perhaps it was because he had no affection for anyone, that he took everything and gave nothing in return. Whatever the reason, the cat still brings back vivid memories of the life that we used to lead, and we often wonder if he is still alive somewhere up there in the north.

I had hardly eased myself out of the driving seat when the three-legged cat appeared. He really was a disgusting animal with a spiteful nature, blotchy brown fur and one of his front legs missing. Even Maggie, who loved all animals, had been heard to say that the vet should have kept the leg and destroyed the cat. He lived three or four doors away and ever since we moved in had adopted the habit of sleeping underneath my car. He would disappear some time in the small hours, leaving behind him a trail of crooked pawmarks and a terrible smell.

Tonight he went through his usual routine, springing up on to the boot of the car and from there on to the roof. Then he clawed his crooked way, skidding and slipping, along the roof, down the windscreen and over the bonnet. Then he disappeared, purring in between the front wheels, under the still warm engine.

I sighed as I looked at the paw marks on the roof. I really must do something about that cat. I closed the garage door, and then as usual, opened it slightly, partly out of consideration for the feline amputee, and partly because of tomorrow's smell. 'I really must do something about it' I told myself. 'Have a word with its owner, or buy some kind of repellent perhaps. I really must find the time.'

That was the story of my life lately, trying to find time. I had built up the business until it was providing Maggie and I with all that we really wanted out of life in the material sense. We had a good home in a modern house, food, clothes, comfort. But the business was eating our lives away. We never really got away from it, never had time for anything else, for living life for its own sake. Time and money. Money and time. It seemed that if you wanted the one, you couldn't have the other.

The phone was ringing as I stepped over the threshold. It rang twice as we were eating, and three times again during the next hour.

'Trouble up at t'mill,' I said to Maggie, as I put the phone down for the last time. 'I don't know why we put up with it. Why we don't sell up and move to somewhere rural and peaceful and be content with a living wage and a simple way of life?'

I had said the same, or something very much like it, a hundred times before, and Maggie and I had often dreamed of life in one of the sleepy little villages of Norfolk, our favourite holiday county. We had always come back to earth though. We had always known that we were city people, and would have been completely out of place in such a setting. So we had always agreed. But this time it was different, and the difference was in Maggie's attitude. She put down her sewing very carefully and turned in her chair slightly so that she was looking straight at me.

'All right,' she said, 'we will.'

8

'Will what?' I asked, alarmed at her unusually intense expression.

Maggie didn't answer, but gravely passed me a newspaper, carefully folded, and with one advert heavily ringed in biro.

'For sale,' I read, 'in rural Norfolk. Village Post Office and general store, Detached property set in one acre.'

The advert went on to give details of turnover, Post Office salary, etc. Maggie waited for me to speak.

'Oh, er, it sounds very nice,' I said. 'Very rural and peaceful, but it's not the kind of thing that would really interest us, is it?'

'Why not?' said Maggie.

'Well, could you see me as a village postmaster for a start?' I laughed.

'Yes,' said Maggie, and she didn't laugh. 'Why not?' she said again.

'Well,' I said, realizing that I was being cornered. 'People just don't.'

Maggie pursed her lips. 'We are not people,' she said, with a woman's logic. 'We are us. Why not?'

I poured a drink, stalling for time while I thought. I tried to bring the conversation on to a less serious level, and laughed.

'What about the smelly three-legged cat?' I asked. 'What would he do if we left?'

'He would do,' said Maggie with emphasis, 'whatever he did before we came. I say that we should try the rural life for a year, and then, if we find that we have made a mistake we can sell up and come back again to the city.'

There was a moment's silence, then Maggie spoke again.

'And to hell with the three-legged cat,' she said.

If I had paused to think about it I would have realized that my reply could have affected the rest of our lives, but I was tired, and anxious to agree with my unusually serious spouse, so I tried to be flippant.

'Right,' I said, and drained my glass with a flourish and banged it down on to the table. 'To hell with the three-legged cat.'

9

The next few weeks flew by as quickly and smoothly as if we were being hastened along by destiny itself, lest we should change our minds. We paid a flying visit to Norfolk and made the vendor an offer which he accepted, and then drove straight back up north and put our house on the market. It was a bad time to sell a house, so we were told, but we had a buyer within a week and he wanted to be in quickly. My time was taken up with packing, talking to accountants, chivying up solicitors, and mainly ensuring that the money required for the purchase of the Post Office stores would be safely in our bank account in time for the completion date. My shares were offered to a fellow director who snapped them up eagerly, and I didn't have time to feel any remorse at leaving the business that I had spent ten years of my life building up from scratch. The month of December rolled on, and we came to our last Christmas dinner in the house. Neither Maggie nor I had a second thought. We were by now so excited by the home that we were going to that we felt no sadness at all about the home that we were leaving. Around the end of the year we rounded things off nicely by throwing a farewell party for our relatives and friends, and then we packed away all the glasses and china in tea chests.

It wasn't until we were heading south, having left the A1 and negotiated King's Lynn, and were driving down a deserted country lane that led nowhere except into the heart of rural Norfolk that it hit Maggie and I that we had really done it. For better or for worse we were now heading for the rural life, the quiet village, the daydream existence. I stopped the car, and looked at Maggie.

'We've really done it,' I said.

She smiled. 'I know,' she said. 'You can keep all your factories and chimneys, and your motorways and smog. This is what I want to see every day.'

We both looked at the quiet countryside around us.

'Yes,' I agreed. 'To hell with the city.'

'Yes,' said Maggie. 'And to hell with the three-legged cat.'

TWO

JANUARY & FEBRUARY

IT was the beginning of January when we moved in, and although we were prepared for snow and ice the weather deceived us. We had a thunderstorm. I had left Maggie arranging curtains and pictures and set out for my first visit to the village pub just before the storm started. Dashing through the first heavy drops of rain, I burst into the small bar and found the place crowded. Outside, the countryside was dark and dripping, but inside there was light and warmth and cheer.

Suddenly there was an extra loud clap of thunder, and all the lights went out. Behind the bar, George, the landlord, who must have anticipated just such an emergency, produced a flashlight and made a dive for the cellar. The customers had hardly had time to start complaining before he reappeared carrying a large plank which he placed on the bar. The plank had two car headlamps attached to it, one at either end, and two wires ran from these. In less time than it takes to tell, George connected the wires to a twelve volt car battery beneath the bar, then he flicked a switch. The bar was bathed in light as two beams of painful intensity split the darkness.

'Now, how's that, gents?' asked George, beaming.

At the far end of the bar, directly in the glare of the headlamps, an elderly man struggled to his feet, shielding his eyes from the light. He later turned out to be Percy, one of the village's best-known characters.

'Very nice, George,' the man said, groping blindly between the tables. 'Very nice I'm sure. I should dip 'em though if I were you, you never know, you might meet another blarsted pub coming the other way.' And he slammed the door loudly as he left.

I first spoke to Percy on my second visit to the pub. On the night of the thunderstorm I had left shortly after the old man and dashed back to the Post Office, knowing that Maggie was frightened of thunder. Now on my second visit I was prepared for a leisurely couple of drinks and any local company that might offer itself. I stepped through the old oak door into the new world that we had chosen to live in. The strangers who were to be our neighbours had soft sounding accents, and wore tweed jackets and fishermen's jerseys, and Norfolk jackets, and polished leather boots. They had tanned faces and a wholesome soap-and-water look about them, and I was uncomfortably aware of my lightweight suit and my office pallor.

As I turned from the bar my elbow caught a glass, tipping it over and spilling the contents. It was one of those tiny slim glasses that are used for serving a particular brand of liqueur whisky, one of the most expensive drinks in the house. The glass belonged to old Percy. He waved aside my apology with a chuckle, but readily accepted the replacement drink that I bought.

'It's an ill wind,' he commented. 'Anyway, it's got us a-mardlin'.'

Mardlin', I was to learn, was the locals' term for chatting, or gossiping, and mardle we did. As we did so I found myself liking the old boy. From the toes of his boots, like two chestnuts freshly split from their shells, to the top of his brilliantine-soaked head, he radiated a childlike naïvety, and by the time that we parted company I felt as though I had known Percy for years.

It was on a later visit that Percy and I were sitting in the bar, the old man with his usual two glasses in front of him, the half tankard of beer and the elegant liqueur glass. The door opened and a stranger entered.

Percy nudged me. 'That'll be the new feller, the one who's bought Mill Cottage,' he said. 'I'd best go and christen him.'

Standing, he drained his liqueur at a gulp, and then topped up the small glass from his tankard of beer. Then he crossed to the bar and positioned himself close to the stranger. The old man stared straight ahead, as if he had suddenly discovered something fascinating about the ancient woodworm-riddled shelf behind the bar. But his hand was slowly moving, sliding the glass towards the stranger's elbow. It was beautifully done. As the man turned he knocked the glass. It was tipped but not broken. Percy accepted the drink that was offered, and the two were soon deep in conversation. When I slipped out of the door they were a-mardlin' as though they had known each other for years, the stranger with a look of respect for his new-found friend, and Percy with his air of almost childlike innocence.

When it came to the running of the business, small problems arose as soon as we moved in. Being absolutely inexperienced in the retail trade, Maggie and I had done considerable homework before we opened. We had taken over the kind of shop that sold everything from baked beans to galvanized buckets, from tin tacks to toffee bars, and we also had the problem of the local dialect. We knew that if a housewife asked for a 'dwile' she meant a floorcloth, and if she said 'cert' she meant suet, but we were completely mystified when a young farmer asked for 'That there harnser over there.' When the harnser turned out to be a picture postcard with a photograph of a heron on it, we were no wiser.

'Can you tell me,' I asked him, 'why is a heron called a harnser?'

'Yes,' was the reply. 'If you can tell me why a harnser is called a heron where you come from.'

Then there was one morning when a dear little old lady smiled up at me sweetly and asked me for what sounded like 'a dust pun'.

'Ah yes,' I said, and showed her a galvanized dust bin. The old dear looked at me as though I were insane.

'That's a dust bin,' she said.

'Oh, I'm sorry,' I said, and quickly produced a dust pan, complete with brush.

She goggled at me, her neck reddening. 'That,' she snapped, 'is a dust pan.'

Clucking to herself, she turned her back on me and started rummaging through the stock, banging things down on the shelves and muttering. Requests to her to describe the mysterious 'dust pun' were ignored. Then I made a terrible mistake. I asked her, in all innocence, to spell 'dust pun'. The sweet little old lady was instantly transformed into a sinewy amazon with veins pulsing at her temples.

'I may not be able to spell "dust pun",' she snarled, 'but there are some ignorant foreigners around here who wouldn't even know a dust pun if they fell over one.'

She turned and stormed towards the door, and then suddenly stopped in her tracks. She stooped and picked up one of those narrow black-painted shovels that are used for removing the ashes from fireplaces. She rumbled towards me, brandishing the shovel, her face a mask of rage.

'She's going to attack me,' I thought. 'Her mind's snapped.'

I backed away until I was pressed hard up against the counter. I considered for a split second the possibility of leaping over the counter, but dismissed the idea. With the amount of andrenalin surging through her veins that she now had, the old lady could probably jump farther than I could anyway. She came to a halt in front of me and waved the shovel within an inch of my nose.

'This,' she bawled hoarsely, 'is a dust pun.'

Ben was the opposite of Percy in appearance, but was none the less a character for that. Where Percy was polished and scrubbed, Ben was ragged and grimy. I never saw Ben with a beard, but I never saw Ben with a shave. How he always managed to be wearing a three day stubble I can't imagine, but he did, and Ben wouldn't have been Ben without it. Short and squat, wearing a battered old trilby with a turned down brim and a sports coat two sizes too big for him, Ben had a cartoon character appearance that made him stand out in any crowd. His visits to the Post Office each Thursday to draw his pension was one of the highlights of Ben's week. Although he worked regularly and hard, as did most retired men in the village, he was officially at least, a pensioner. On his weekly visits he would pull my leg unmercifully, and however ridiculous the argument that he led me into, he was always the winner. He would adopt the broadest possible Norfolk accent and ask me for unheard of herbal remedies, or a particular brand of liniment (rubbin licker he called it), and then would profess astonishment when told that we didn't stock the stuff. One day I was serving him with a few odds and ends.

'Your drawing pins, Ben,' I said.

'Oh no, bor,' he said, 'you don't say it right. Drorin pins is what they are.'

'Ben, you old devil,' I said, 'I'm not going to argue with you. You can call them what you like, but they are drawing pins.'

I should have known better. Leaning himself against a shelf to take the weight off his game leg, Ben prepared himself for a long and enjoyable dispute. I looked round in desperation. A young man had entered behind Ben and was waiting to be served. From the man's dark suit I judged him to be a salesman of some sort, and therefore a potential ally, so I brought him into the conversation.

'Please tell me,' I begged him, 'what would you call these.' I held up the drawing pins.

'Well,' drawled the man, in a strong American accent, 'I'd call them thumb tacks.'

Ben collapsed, wheezing with laughter.

After several weeks of the rural life Maggie and I had become quite accustomed to the sight of rabbits on the lawn, squirrels in the orchard and the odd fox crossing the lane. We began to think of ourselves as quite knowledgeable country folk, and filled letters to relatives with little stories of our country life.

One early closing day the weather turned suddenly quite warm and spring-like, and we decided to risk it and have tea outside on the lawn for the first time. We were commenting on the imminence of spring and the promised beauty of the countryside, when our attention was drawn to a rustling in the shrubbery. As we went to investigate, we were startled when the leaves parted and we saw a savage pointed face staring up at us. We had seen weasels now and then, and stoats, but this animal was far too big to be one of them, what the devil could it be? Were there animals abroad that Maggie and I had never even heard of? The creature took a step towards us, and we took a hasty step back. Then it stepped out on to the grass, in full view. Great Heavens, it was bigger than a large cat, bigger than a dog probably. It was a sinuous, light brown monster and it stood there confidently, sniffing at us with that long pointed nose. Slowly we backed to the door of the house, the thing slowly following, and when we reached the door we shot inside, then slammed the door and bolted it. Through the closed window we watched the animal as it slowly examined our sandwiches, and for the first time I wished that I had taken the villagers' advice and bought myself a shotgun. Then suddenly a short, whiskery figure burst through the shrubbery and trundled across the lawn. It was Ben.

'I've bin a-lookin' all over for this blarsted ferret,' he called, and seized the animal by the scruff of the neck. Then stuffing the creature down the front of his shirt, next to his skin, he waved and limped away.

About once every two months or so we were visited by a pensioner from the nearby village. His name was Naseby, and we were favoured with his custom after he had some sort of disagreement with his own village sub-postmaster. Mrs Finch was serving in the shop when Mr Naseby made his first visit and my attention was drawn to the man by the squeak of muffled laughter that came from our assistant, who often had trouble controlling herself when something triggered off her keen sense of the ridiculous. One look at the customer and the reason for her hilarity became obvious. It was a good thing for us that the man was slightly deaf, or he might have been as annoyed with us as he said he was with the proprietor of the shop in his village. Mr Naseby had the biggest nose that I have ever seen in my life. It wasn't the red-veined nose of the hardened drinker or swollen or enlarged in any way, but it was at least twice as big as it ought to have been, and it gave Mr Naseby a most comical appearance, rather like one of those toucans or hornbills that one sees in zoos. After I had dealt with him at the Post Office end of the store, Mr Naseby moved along to where Mrs Finch was waiting, and started browsing along the shelves.

'I'm looking for a small present that would be suitable for a pensioner very much like myself,' he said.

'How about a box of handkerchiefs?' asked Mrs Finch, staring mesmerized at the nose now in close-up.

'No,' said Mr Naseby, 'that's a bit too ordinary. I want something a bit different.'

I reached out and caught Mrs Finch's hand as she was reaching for a tray full of tins of snuff, and diverted her attention to a box full of tie pins and cuff links. Mr Naseby sorted through the box, cocking the enormous nose to one side just like some kind of great bird.

'I think I'll take this,' he said, picking out a tie pin with a small gilt pheasant on it.

'Good,' said Mrs Finch, still watching the nose as if she expected it to do something. She wrapped the purchase and handed it to him.

'Thank you, Mr Noseby,' she said.

I felt that I had to butt in at that point and I tried to break Mrs Finch's train of thought by asking the man how it had come about that he had fallen out with his own village shop-keeper. Naseby scowled, wrinkling the nose in the process.

'He's too darned rude,' he said, 'too abrupt, and always in a hurry to get rid of you.' He sniffed loudly, and Mrs Finch held on to the box of tie pins as if to prevent them being drawn into the air.

'Another thing,' said Naseby, starting to chuckle 'the fellow hardly looks human. He's got the biggest pair of ears that you've ever seen in your life.' He laughed heartily, the nose snorting intermittently as if it had a sense of humour all of its own. Mrs Finch, glad of an excuse to relieve her own pent-up laughter, joined in, and the two of them howled together in the most unmusical duet.

'Oh, blarst me,' said Mr Naseby, 'I know that we shouldn't laugh at folk, but they are such great big things, and doesn't he look funny.'

He laughed again, and wiped away the tears that were coursing down each side of the great nose. 'Oh, dear,' he said, exhausted, 'thare are some queer-looking people about, and that's for sure.'

18

Whenever complaints about poaching in the area reached a certain level, it was normal procedure for our young village policeman to receive reinforcements in the shape of P.C. Danby. Danby was a middle-aged man from a larger village nearby. He could smell a poacher half a mile away, and in fact thought like a poacher himself, and when he was investigating in the area, Len, the only professional poacher in the village, had the choice of taking a rest from his nocturnal occupation or being caught.

Len didn't object to this arrangement, as Danby removed any amateur competitors from Len's patch, and Len had a good deal of respect for Danby.

It was while P.C. Danby's car was parked in a small recess in the bushes of the copse on Young 'Enry's land that 'Enry himself burst out of the trees and dashed up to him. Although it was only just daylight Young 'Enry was wide awake, in fact he was breathless and red in the face from exertion.

'Arrest him,' he panted. 'Arrest him. I caught him red-handed.'

Danby climbed slowly out of the car, his face impassive.

'Been going on for weeks,' shouted Young 'Enry, waving his arms about. 'Shots in the night, traps and snares on my land, and not a thing being done about it.'

Danby listened to him politely, his arms crossed on his chest, his head on one side. He said not a word. Then Len appeared. He strolled out of the trees, a straw in his mouth, and whistling softly to himself.

'I was just getting out of bed,' said 'Enry, 'when I heard these two shots. I ran all the way, and found him.' He jerked his head towards Len, who was idly examining the police car.

'Mornin',' said Len, and nodded to Danby in a friendly fashion.

'There were feathers,' said Young 'Enry, his voice rising almost to a falsetto, 'pheasant feathers all over the place.'

Len grinned at him. 'Mebbe it's the time o' year,' he said.

Danby appeared to rouse himself with an effort, like a man reluctant to wake up from a pleasant dream.

'Are you accusing this man of poaching on your property?' he asked.

Young 'Enry choked, and quivered from head to foot, 'Of course I am,' he yelled. 'What the devil do you think I've just been telling you about?'

'Well, sir,' said Danby in his most official manner, 'what proof do you have? Did the man have a gun in his possession, or a bird perhaps?'

Young 'Enry gurgled.

'Did he have the bird that you claim was shot?' went on Danby.

'Enry was now dancing up and down with rage, and when he spoke it was with difficulty. His voice came out in a strangled squeak.

'He's hidden it, hasn't he?' he said. 'You come with me to where I found him and you'll find a gun and a bird or two hidden somewhere. You know where to look, you've done that kind of thing before.'

Danby looked at 'Enry with a thoughful frown, but didn't move.

'I'll get a dog,' said 'Enry. 'Wait here and I'll get a gun dog; he'll sniff 'em out for sure.'

'You can borrow mine if you like,' said Len generously, smiling. The big old labrador was lying a few yards away, his head on his paws, his eyes watching Len's every move.

'It seems to me, sir,' said Danby with elaborate politeness, 'that this, er, gentleman here is guilty of trespassing on your land while taking his dog for an early morning walk. Without asking headquarters to take men from other more important duties, in order to scour the countryside, I doubt whether proof of any other illegal act could be found.' He checked the button on his breast pocket as he spoke, as if to signify that his notebook wouldn't be required. 'Now, as to this trespassing. Did the man leave your property quietly when asked to do so?'

Young 'Enry couldn't believe his ears. Danby, the poacher's arch enemy, was actually talking Len out of trouble, instead of prosecuting him like the pest he was.

'I didn't ask him to leave,' he shouted at the policeman. 'I saw your car and ran straight to you.'

'Ah, I see sir, so he left your land of his own free will?'

Young 'Enry was speechless.

'There's not a lot I can do in an affair of this nature,' he said. 'A charge of trespass is the only one that you could bring, and I hardly think that it would be worth it in the circumstances.' He gave Len a long hard look as he climbed slowly back into his car. 'I've no doubt at all that we shall meet again though,' he said, 'and next time things might be a bit different.'

When Young 'Enry told the story to Maggie and me later that day in the Post Office, we managed to keep our faces straight and look suitably sympathetic. His account of P.C. Danby's behaviour fitted in perfectly with something that I had seen earlier that morning, before I had opened up the shop. I was standing on top of a tall stepladder, cleaning the shop sign, when Danby drew up in his car. He bade me a cheery 'Good morning' and posted a couple of letters in the box. From my vantage point on top of the steps I could see through the windows and into the back of the police car. On the floor, in front of the rear seats, I had clearly seen a shotgun, and a brace of fine cock pheasants.

John, Ben's only son, was known as the strongest man in our village and for many miles around. Not much taller than his father, but almost twice his fighting weight, John was an impressive figure; but although nature had endowed him with phenomenal muscles, he lacked his father's natural wit, and was more likely to be the butt of any joke rather than the joker.

One of John's favourite demonstrations of his strength, particularly on Saturday nights with more than a gallon of best bitter inside him, was to lift Hubby's pony clean off its feet. He could manage this by squatting beneath the animal, his head between its forelegs, and heaving upwards. He would only attempt this when the pony was harnessed between the shafts of the trap, and doubtless the trap itself tended to lever the animal upwards and off the ground; but nevertheless, it was still a considerable feat. What the pony thought of this performance we could only guess, but it was usually rewarded with a pint of ale, which it obviously enjoyed.

One night in the bar, after his friends had been plying him with pints, and betting him even more pints that he couldn't lift the pony high enough for a brick to be slipped under each of its four hoofs, John spat on his hands and rolled up his sleeves in preparation for the contest. Dr John, our local G.P., who was in the snug, called out to John through the hatchway.

'It's a foolish thing to attempt,' he said. 'That kind of thing can easily lead to a rupture, you know.'

'In that case, don't do it,' said Hubby, the owner of the pony. 'I don't want anything to happen to that pony of mine.'

As far as the youngsters of the village were concerned, Hubby and his pony had always been fair game. Their pranks varied from painting the poor animal in various bright colours while Hubby was busy at the bar, to tying a block to one of the wheels of the trap so that the inebriated Hubby bobbed violently up and down on the journey home, complaining bitterly and loudly about the state that Teddy Collins (the local council's road foreman) had left the road in.

Norfolk jacket, knee breeches and flat cap were Hubby's uniform, and the pony and trap his only means of transport. He was usually the first one through the door of the village pub when it opened, and one of the very last to leave when it closed. The fact that by that time Hubby was quite incapable of driving himself home was no problem at all. The patient little animal would plod its way along the lanes at a steady pace, with Hubby snoring in the back.

On one occasion the youngsters had led the pony away from the fence at the side of the pub and to the nearest gateway. After pushing the shafts of the trap through the five barred gate, they had harnessed up the pony again, leaving the trap on one side of the gate and the pony on the other.

We were told that at closing time, after staggering around in the darkness for some time, Hubby had found the trap and had thrown himself into the back of it, grunting 'Gee up' to the pony. The trap rocked for a few moments as the pony tried to obey, and under the impression that they were moving, Hubby fell asleep. Waking up some time later and weighing up the situation, Hubby had turned to the pony and demanded, 'How the hell did you do that?'

In general though, Hubby's drive home was uneventful, and the routine had worked well for him for years. Then one night a police Panda car, off its usual beat, met Hubby and pony, homeward bound. Realizing that the lane was not wide enough for both trap and car, and that the pony was not going to stop, the policeman braked and swerved. The Panda car rolled over into the ditch.

In court, when asked if he had anything to say, Hubby shrugged his shoulders.

'I was asleep, yer Honour, and the pony can't have been very wide awake.'

The magistrate looked sternly at Hubby. 'It's perfectly obvious to me,' he said, 'that the main contributory factor in this incident was drink.'

'Oh no, yer Honour,' Hubby protested, 'The old pony never has more than a couple of pints a night.'

Another character who visited both the Post Office and the village pub was Buddy. At first I used to get confused between Buddy and Hubby, because of the similarity of their names, but after meeting both of them the confusion ceased, as they were entirely different people. Buddy lived in a nearby larger village, but did all his drinking in our village pub, and all his drinking meant an awful lot of drinking. It was always said that Buddy had been barred from his own local but we never knew why, and as he never gave any trouble at all at first, George made him welcome. Buddy was big and well-built, but always stood badly, and seemed somehow as if he was ready to slump over and fall asleep, even before he had had a drink. He drank like a fish. On his long journey home to the next village, on the unlit country roads, he had had more than one dangerous experience. He had once fallen into a ditch, his bike on top of him in a tangle, and the ditch being warm and dry, had fallen asleep. After a heavy overnight shower he had awakened as the ditch began to fill, and had all but drowned as he struggled with his bike. The game-keeper who came to his help had been attracted to the ditch, not by Buddy's cries for help, but by the sight of several large rats fleeing the ditch at three o'clock in the morning, and when Buddy's head had first appeared in the gloom it had received a blow from the keeper's stick that had sent his false teeth flying out of his mouth.

'What was that for,' asked Buddy after he had been helped to his feet.

'Sorry,' said the keeper, 'I thought you was a rat.'

'Do I look like a ruddy rat? asked Buddy, rubbing his head with a muddy hand.

'You do now that you've lost your teeth,' said the game-keeper.

Buddy had a rubbery sort of face, and large pop eyes. When his teeth were removed his whole face seemed to collapse, and although by no means a handsome man with his teeth in, he was positively repulsive with them out. He had broken his teeth so often when drunk that the authorities now made him pay the full cost of replacements. Buddy's son, who was married, lived in the city, and his job had some-thing to do with a foundry. When Buddy appalled at the cost of keeping a set of teeth in his head, looked for an answer to his problem, his son's occupation came to mind. He per-suaded his son to take his top set to work and have a replica of them cast in aluminium alloy. Armed with these frighten-ing fangs. Buddy drank away, happily secure in the knowl-edge that although he might drop these teeth as often as he dropped the old ones, they would not easily break. He even lost them on the journey home one night, and found them intact in the lane on his journey to the pub the next evening.

In the village pub one night, when one unsuspecting visitor remarked to his female companion, on hearing a loud crash from somewhere behind the bar that 'Somebody has dropped his false teeth', Buddy butted into the conversation eagerly. The lady shrank away as he thrust his rubbery face towards them.

'They started that saying about me, you know,' said Buddy, smiling metallically. The couple gasped as they caught a flash of the famous teeth. 'It used to be, "Buddy's dropped his false teeth", 'cos mine make such a row, look.'

He removed the awful fangs, and the visitors cringed as they saw the rubbery features now devoid of any support. Buddy threw the teeth on to the top of the table with an almighty crash, and they bounced off straight into the lady's lap. She screamed at the top of her voice, and her companion sprang to his feet, upsetting all the drinks as he did so. For the first time we began to see why Buddy had been barred from his own village pub.

Ben trundled into the Post Office and I braced myself for the usual ordeal. On his previous visit the old devil had had a queue of pensioners laughing themselves silly at my expense, and had ended his performance by asking, in the broadest possible Norfolk, for some soup.

'I'll have to be off, so give me a bit o' soup will you,' he said.

I asked him whether he would like beef, chicken or lentil soup. Would he like it in a tin, in a packet, or in a cube.

'Oh no bor, don't start again,' Ben had wheezed. 'Enough for one day, just give me a bar o' carbolic soup and I'll be off.'

His visit this time was different, though. He was already wheezing with laughter as he came through the door, his old face the colour of a ripe plum, and we had to allow him several minutes to recover before we could find out the cause of his merriment. When he eventually regained control of himself he reminded us of the free snacks that were available at the village pub. George the landlord, had recently started serving these snacks at lunchtimes by way of an experiment. A jar of pickled onions was left on the counter, and anyone who had bought a sandwich was invited to help themselves. The older members of the community such as Ben, Charlie and Percy, had soon found that they were on to a good thing. They would drop in for a half pint of beer, and buy one cheese sandwich between them. Then they would help themselves to as many pickled onions as their systems could possibly accommodate. At this rate I couldn't see George allowing the experiment to continue for very much longer.

Eating certain foods presented something of a problem to Ben. He had only one tooth in his head, and this solitary incisor resembled a deformed carrot, both in colour and shape. But Ben wasn't one to miss out when anything was going free, and if he couldn't eat a pickled onion, he could suck it. This he did, with a noise like a sink being unblocked. He rolled the onions around in his mouth, and screwed his eyes up with pleasure. When at length he spat the onions out into the ash tray, there wasn't a drop of vinegar left in them.

On this occasion Ben had come for his pension straight from the pub where, finding himself alone in the bar, he had helped himself to half a dozen pickled onions, emptying the jar. As Ben had left, Young 'Enry had been going into the bar, and while sipping his beer and reading his newspaper had eaten every one of the discarded onions from the tray by his elbow. Ben had seen this, watching through the taproom window, and he wheezed with laughter until his face was purple again as he told us of the incident.

'Gaw bless me,' he gasped, 'Wot a larf. Mind you, ter-morrer should be funnier still.'

'Why should it?' he was asked.

'Becos,' Ben gasped, his eyes streaming, 'if Young 'Enry's there termorrer, I'm a-goin' to tell him.'

Sidney was a well-built youth with a shock of red hair. He lived with his quiet parents in a quiet house near the village church. He was without any doubt the shyest lad in the village and would blush to the roots of his hair whenever anyone spoke to him. Women embarrassed him painfully and Mrs Finch and Maggie would always stand back and let me serve Sidney when he made one of his rare visits to the Post Office. He didn't mix at all, not even with youngsters of his own age, and Maggie and I always felt rather sorry for Sidney.

When the rumours first started in the village, Maggie and I didn't believe them. The stories all varied from each other in detail, but they all had one thing in common. People claimed on many a moonlit night a male figure could be seen running through the village, stark naked.

Though we dismissed the stories as the result of a night's over-indulgence at the bar, or a tale deliberately invented by the young pranksters, when several of the more sober members of the community claimed to have seen the naked runner, we began to wonder. When Miss Money told us herself that she had seen him, we simply had to believe it. Miss Money was a spinster of around sixty and was regarded by all as a pillar of virtue. She was a small, round-faced likeable person who took Sunday school classes and spent the whole of her life in the service of the church and the village. She had never been heard to utter a bad word about anyone, and if she had had her way every prison in the country would have been emptied and the prisoners sent off on long recuperative holidays.

She had been woken up, Miss Money said, by a mouse gnawing in the false roof. Glancing out of the bedroom window she had seen a figure, wearing nothing but a Balaclava helmet, go trotting down the street. He had turned into a field and she had lost sight of him.

'It was bright moonlight,' she said. 'It was a naked man all right.' There was genuine concern in her eyes. 'I've never seen anything like it in my life,' she said, and then added quietly to herself, 'Well, not for an awful long time anyway.'

If anyone in the village was likely to know the truth about the prowler, it was Len. Len was the village poacher. The police knew it, and from time to time Len had slipped up and been caught, but this had not deterred him. He was too old a dog to learn new tricks, and he carried on with his profession, growing more and more expert year by year, and more and more difficult to catch. He spent the best part of each day dozing in the sun if the day was fine, and stretched out on the hearthrug in front of the fire if it was not. The nights were Len's working hours.

I tried several times to contact Len to find out if he had any information as to the identity of the naked runner, but before I could do so the matter resolved itself.

In the small hours of the morning Maggie and I were awakened by the sound of a gunshot from somewhere pretty close to the Post Office. I grabbed my trousers and a torch and had a good look around outside, but saw no one. In the shop the next morning the grapevine by which news travels around the village was saying that Dr John had been called out in the middle of the night, and the house that he had been called to was the home of young Sidney. We never saw Sydney again after that. His parents told us some time afterwards that he had joined the army as a boy soldier. His father said that it was the best thing that he could have done, and we agreed with him, thinking that the life would do him the world of good.

My repeated attempts to get Dr John to reveal the identity of his night-time patient were unsuccessful, even in the congenial atmosphere of the pub, but he did seem to smile into his beer a lot whenever I brought the matter up.

Sometime after the affair, I was buying a secondhand shotgun from Len, and I quizzed him about the incident. The village seemed to have forgotten all about the naked prowler and I said that there would be no harm in his sharing any secret that he might have. Len denied all knowledge of the runner, or that he had even seen him, but like Dr John, he seemed to get a great deal of amusement from his own thoughts. I mentioned the night of the gunshot close to the Post Office, and he grinned.

'I remember that,' he said. 'Hope I didn't spoil your dreams. It was like this. There was this great big white goose, you see. I saw him-a-wandering around your orchard. Now I didn't want to go and kill him, did I? He did belong to somebody in the village after all, he was just strayin' a bit you might say. But on the other hand I couldn't leave him to get up to his mischief while all you good folk were abed.

So I lets him get very nearly out of range,' he said, shaking with laughter, 'And then I sort of peppers him, very gently. Makes a good target, stands out lovely and white on a moonlit night a big white goose does.'

'Oh I see,' I said. 'And what happened to this goose after that, did it fly away?'

'No,' said Len, laughing aloud at the picture in his mind. 'Not right then and there it didn't, but it did clear a couple of pretty high hedges.'

THREE

MARCH & APRIL

THE weather was now improving daily and Maggie and I got into the habit of taking regular walks around the country lanes after closing the shop. It was on these walks that we met many local characters who did not come into the Post Office very often, and having plenty of time to spare, we would always stop and listen to any tales that were likely to be told. One such story was the one about the bog oak.

In rural areas of Norfolk, particularly on the farms, many items can be found that are made from a particularly hard and heavy type of wood. Not being well up in such matters, I had always assumed that they were made from some foreign timber that had been imported in quantity in times gone by. I was corrected in this assumption by the village carpenter and joiner. The wood was bog oak, he said. Bog oak was simply ordinary oak that had been felled and then buried for some time in a bog or waterlogged land. It was often left buried for years, as many people believed that the longer it remained buried, the better the quality of the timber when it was eventually used.

'Adam Higgs,' said the carpenter, 'He was the boy for bog oak. He lived way back before my time and used to have that smallholding that the Higgs's have today. Now old Adam was a man who was certain that he was going to live for ever, and lived his life accordingly. At ninety he planted a field with acorns, saying that oak was going to be scarce in the future, and he would make himself a fortune when the trees were big enough to be felled. When he was near on a hundred he buried a great load of bog oak in the wet meadows near the stream, saying that he might need the money later on in life. It must have been a heck of a load of timber, as I've been told by more than one old timer that it took a team of horses nigh on a week to cart it to his place. They say that the old man could be seen working till well past midnight for weeks, burying the stuff. The trouble is that boundaries have changed such a lot since those days, and no one knows just where the stuff was buried. The old man didn't leave any records you see, he didn't think that he was going.'

'But he did die after all?' I asked.

The carpenter laughed. 'Oh yes, he died all right, just as we all will, and the stuff was forgotten for a whole generation, what with the war and all. Then his grandson, the present Higgs, took over the place. He started searching for the timber right away, prices being what they are, but he was touchy about it though, and wouldn't admit to what he was doing. At one time he had half the university down at his place, searching for Roman relics, and torcs and things. They didn't find any relics. And they didn't find any bog oak either. The family can still be seen on occasions, digging out a badger where there hasn't been a badger on their land for a hundred years, 'cos of the wet, or sometimes driving long poles into the ground. That's to discourage moles, so they say. I reckon young Higgs is as odd as his old grandad was.'

'And the oak still lies buried somewhere?' I asked.

'Yes,' he said, 'and in my opinion it won't be found by searching for it. I think that the stream has shifted its course slowly over the years and the timber is probably right under the water.'

'And what about the old man,' I asked. 'How did old Adam die in the end?'

'Well it wasn't of old age,' said the carpenter. 'He was fit and active right up to the end, buying and felling timber, sawing and selling it, and working his bit of land as well. He was over a hundred, and was supervising the loading of some timber that he had sold. The load slipped and he was crushed. Funny thing too, it was a great baulk of bog oak that did for him.'

Cecil Pipes used to talk to machines. Known to all simply as 'Pipes' he had done a part-time postman's job for years, working from around five thirty in the morning until around eleven or so. During the second half of the day he worked as a machine operator for a small local firm that manufactured breeze blocks. His job entailed the operation and mainten- ance of a petrol driven cement mixer of gigantic proportions. Pipes spent the afternoons of each working day standing at the side of this great machine, his head cocked to one side, listening to its mechanical heart beating, and talking to it. Pipes had to time the mixing, and when it was finished turn a huge handwheel, which tipped the contents of the machine into a hopper, from whence it would splodge its way down to the block-making equipment on the floor below. Then he would reverse the mouth of the monster so that a workmate, standing on a platform at shoulder height to Pipes, could shovel in the ingredients for the next mix. His firm thought very highly of Pipes and it was a well-known fact that the machinery would not run nearly so well when Pipes was absent. He vowed that if a person was not in sympathy with a machine, or that if he let a machine know that he didn't like it, it would break down out of sheer cussedness.

'Every machine has a mind of its own,' he used to say. 'After all, they are only human.'

I used to smile at this, but one day something happened that almost convinced me that Pipes was right after all. Almost, but not quite. I had received a query concerning a parcel that Pipes had delivered on his morning round, and as things were pretty quiet in the store I took a stroll round to the yard where he was working. As we talked the giant mixer puttered and popped away in the background. Suddenly it stopped.

'Must be finishing time,' said Pipes. 'The old girl always

knows when its five thirty, folk won't believe it but it's true.'

I checked my watch. It was five thirty all right, give or take a minute or two. The sudden silencing of the machine had been so dramatic that Pipes almost had me believing his theory about mechanical things, but as I watched him tipping the last load of the day out of the mixer something in the corner caught my eye. It was a bucket, and carefully painted around the inside were three lines. These lines had numbers painted on them. Four thirty, five, and on the top line, five thirty. Above this line there was one word painted. It said 'Overtime'. I picked up the bucket and sniffed. It smelt of petrol.

Of all the people in the village, John, Ben's muscular son, was the last one that you would have thought of as a business man. It's not surprising therefore, that eyebrows were raised when John announced to the world in general that he was going into business.

'Goats,' he said. 'That's where the money is, in goats.'

Several people in the village kept the odd goat, and a great number of people drove out from the city on Sunday mornings to buy goat's milk. How true it is I do not know, but many people bought the milk in the belief that it would cure a great number of ailments, from eczema, asthma and hay fever, to headaches and chilblains. The goat itself was treated by the villagers with a respect that seemed to Maggie and I to be the remnants of some age-old superstition. The locals were never specific as to how the goat differed from other animals, but in the same way as they referred to a blackthorn as 'a quare old tree', so they referred to the goat as 'a quare old animal'.

John was absolutely certain of the fortune that awaited him. He would breed goats and sell the kids. He would charge high stud fees, once he had made his name. He would sell vast quantities of milk in the city, once he had established his contacts. He started off his business career by buying one very large, very old billy goat.

On any fine day the shop door stood open all day long. A

few strips of coloured tape hung in the doorway and acted as a fly screen, and these rustled whenever a customer entered.

Tuesday mornings were always rather quiet around ten thirty, and I was taking the opportunity to grab a cup of tea in the stockroom when I heard the fly screen rustle. I stepped quickly into the shop and found myself face to face with a large and smelly goat. The animal chewed thoughtfully as it weighed me up. Mrs Finch, our assistant, gave me a frightened squeak from the stockroom as she caught sight of the goat, and he shook his head at her and waggled his horns by way of reply.

Bracing myself I walked boldly up to him and said, 'Shoo, off you go.'

The goat tilted its head on one side and fixed me with one pale eye. I swallowed, and tried not to show the fear I was feeling. I grabbed an apple from the display and held it out.

'Here boy,' I said, 'nice apple.'

The goat stretched his neck and reached towards me. He ignored the apple and started nibbling at my sleeve. I dropped the apple and taking hold of the short length of chain that hung from the animal's collar, I tried to lead him towards the door. He didn't move one inch. I then tried to drag him, leaning my weight on the chain. The goat leaned the other way. As he did so he lowered his head. Thinking that he was going to charge, I let go of the chain and took refuge behind the postcard stand. But the goat didn't charge. Instead he retreated. As he did so his rear end crashed into a shelf, sending tins flying in all directions. The goat then turned round to see what had caused all the noise, and as he did so his tail end knocked over a tray of apples. This started off a sequence of events that could conceivably have carried on indefinitely. Each time that he turned round to see what had happened behind him, his rump knocked something else to the floor. Each time he knocked something to the floor, he turned round to have a look. Not being at all experienced where goats were concerned, I had assumed that any damage that was going to be done was going to be caused by the dangerous looking horns on the beast's head, and yet here was

34

this goat, demolishing the premises with that end of its anatomy that didn't have any horns. At one point, as I was pursuing the goat through a welter of tomatoes, apples and tinned sardines, Percy's face appeared for a fleeting minute through the fly screen. I learnt later that it had been he who called in the cavalry to my assistance. The goat had just demolished the eggs when John appeared. He grabbed the goat's horns in his big hands and twisted its head sideways. Without a word he led the animal out of the shop, the goat teetering on tiptoe. As he left he had to pass through a crowd of about thirty people who for the past few minutes had been watching spellbound through the window. I am still not sure whether the cheers that rang out were for my rescuer or for the goat.

I had intended to shovel all the debris into cartons and

deliver them to John, together with a bill, but by the time I had cleared up the mess I was beginning to see the funny side of the affair and so I relented. I was glad later that I had, when I heard the rest of the saga of the goat. The Post Office stores had been the last call that he had made on his journey through the village. After chasing George's wife around the pub garden until she had locked herself in the gent's outside toilet, he had ruined two or three gardens in a casual sort of way as he travelled along the village street. Then he had seen Dr John's new car standing at the kerb. Mistaking his own reflection in the door of the car for a rival, he had charged and charged again, and kept on charging until the door swung open and the rival disappeared. Satisfied, he had wandered around to the other side of the car. On the other side there was another door, and in the other door there was another rival. The performance was repeated. When the doctor came to drive his car he found that the two doors were too badly damaged to be repaired, and two new doors were eventually fitted. The damaged gardens had to be paid for. If John wanted to continue living anything like a normal life in the village he had to pay up, regardless of what the law had to say about the matter. In scraping together the money that he had to find, John sent a number of things to the auctioneers. Amongst them was the billy goat.

It was shortly after his appearance in court that the change came over Hubby. He somehow became convinced that he was going to die. Perhaps Dr John had tried to frighten him into giving up drinking by warning him of what might happen. If that was the case then it had exactly the opposite effect. Convinced, in spite of anything that anyone might say, that he had only a very short time left, Hubby set about enjoying himself with a terrible determination. Being a bachelor, he had only himself to consider. He sold his cottage and its five acres, keeping for himself only a very small plot, on which he lived in a modern caravan. He sold the pony and trap, and bought himself a brand new car. He was never seen to drive it himself, being content to allow the many young

36

volunteers to chauffeur him from pub to pub. He discarded his Norfolk jacket and flat cap, and bought himself several smart suits, and he did no work at all.

He ate and smoked and drank as though his life depended on it, instead of the reverse, and swore to anyone who would listen that he wouldn't live until Easter. The days passed by, and Hubby lived on. Easter was almost here. If Hubby lasted longer than he had expected, his money didn't. His visits to the city became less and less frequent. Eventually his shiny new car was sold, and he was left to walk to and from the village pub. He even began to have occasional doubts about the inevitability of his end, and now and again listened to Dr John when he tried to explain that there was no reason at all why Hubby should die. But Hubby usually shook his head sadly, as if he knew something that the doctor did not. He watched the approach of the Easter week-end with misgivings, and after it had come and gone, he was reluctantly convinced. He wasn't going to die after all.

It was a few days after Easter that Maggie and I saw Hubby as we were walking along the lane that ran by his plot. He was working on the small garden that surrounded his caravan and he looked fit and energetic, and had a slight tan. He was wearing his old cap and breeches again. We congratulated him on his return to health, and said that he must now be looking forward to a long and happy life. He agreed with us, but with a trace of reluctance, and I could swear that in his expression there was a look of something very much like disappointment.

The pretty flint cottage that Hubby sold was bought by a family of well-to-do week-enders from the city. The place was in no fit state for them to move into right away, being grimy in places and down right filthy in others. Most of the woodwork seemed to be held together by several coats of bituminous paint, on which the woodworm seemed to thrive. The property was certainly worth spending money on, and a horde of workmen descended on the place. They did excellent work and made the cottage look a picture. The lady of the house, and her teenage daughter moved in as an advance party, and curtains appeared at the windows, and smoke from the chimney. We had an advert in the Post Office window to the effect that a part-time handyman-cum-gardener was required at the cottage, and the rate of pay mentioned seemed quite generous. Ben applied for the job, and the lady interviewed him.

'Oh dear,' she said, when she saw him standing there in the smart new kitchen, swaying slightly on his game leg. His stained old trilby hat was still on his head, and he smelt of something rural and distinctly organic. 'Oh my dear man, I had an altogether different sort of person in mind, if you don't mind my saying so. All my friends seem to find such absolute gems of employees you know. Ruddy cheeks and skilful fingers and all that sort of thing. Absolute founts of wisdom and country lore, if you know what I mean. Oh dear me, what am I to do?'

'Why, do what they do, marm,' said Ben. 'Exaggerate.'

Ben didn't get himself the job, but shortly afterwards found a regular part-time position on Young 'Enry's farm. Young 'Enry was a character in his own right, but not the sort of rural type one expects to find running a farm. Old 'Enry died while Young 'Enry was still in his twenties, and being the only child he had inherited a small but profitable farm. But Young 'Enry's heart was not in farming. A born gambler and follower of the horses, he decided to combine business with pleasure and become a horse breeder. His one ambition in life was to breed a real winner, a horse that would win the Derby or perhaps the Grand National. He established a riding school, and seemed to be making a living out of it, in spite of leaving the running of it to his employees while he concentrated on the pursuit of his great dream. His attempts to breed the horse that would go down in history ran away with quite a lot of the working capital that he had been left, as he spent an enormous sum on the purchase of a young mare and then felt compelled to pay what amounted to a king's ransom by way of a stud fee. The gamble didn't come off. The result of the union was an animal that looked so promising that it appeared to be the answer to Young 'Enry's prayers, but in

38

private gallops even against his old riding hacks it soon became obvious that the horse would never be worth racing. Young 'Enry decided to cut his losses and sell the animal while it was still young, and before the word got around. He assumed that no countryman would be foolish enough to buy his white elephant, especially at the price that he was expecting to get, so he offered it to one of the city business men that he despised so much, one of the group who had formed a syndicate, bought a couple of racehorses, and as Young 'Enry put it 'Wouldn't know which end of the horse to put the bridle on.' A meeting was arranged, and after much haggling during which Young 'Enry refused to lower his extortionate asking price by one penny, the businessman agreed to buy the horse, providing 'Enry threw in the young filly that was the horse's stable mate at the time. The bargain was struck, and they shook hands on it. Young 'Enry chortled around the village for days afterwards at the way he had put it over the city gent. But as time passed his laughter grew fainter and then died. The syndicate never did race his horse, but they did race the young filly, as soon as it was old enough, and it began to win. Time and time again its name would appear amongst the first three past the post, until Young 'Enry could hardly bring himself to read about it. Finally, when he read that the horse had been sold to an American for more than his whole farm would have fetched on the open market, Young 'Enry sold off all his horses, ploughed up his paddocks and went back to farming.

Ben's workmate at Young 'Enry's farm was Shorty Smith. Shorty was six feet seven inches tall, and appeared to be even taller, because he was thinner than any human being deserved to be. Ben, five feet nothing and as broad as he was long, appeared to work well with his odd partner, and there did seem to be a kind of logic in the arrangement. Young 'Enry said that they were quicker at almost any job than any other two workers because each one could do what the other one found difficult.

Whether Shorty's thinness was due to heredity or some illness, we were never sure, but Shorty himself was quite definite on the subject. His lean appearance was due, he said, to a condition that had almost killed him when he had been younger. From being a child, he said, he had been in the habit of picking the ears of growing corn and eating them. He swore that on many a day while working in the fields he had eaten nothing all the day long, save a few handfuls of ripe wheat. Then one day, so he said, a meal of wheat had germinated inside him, and started to grow. Shorty had gone off his food, but had carried on working in the countryman's belief that such a natural phenomenon would soon be righted by Mother Nature herself. But his condition had worsened as the wheat continued to grow. In the end he had been forced to seek medical help. Shorty told us the story many times over, and swore that every detail was the gospel truth.

'I didn't go to the petty for a month or more,' he said. 'Wheat spouted from my backside like a besom broom.' When we didn't express any disbelief he went on. 'I had to go to hospital with one o' mawther's old skirts on, 'cos I couldn't get into a pair of trousers.'

Ignoring Ben's question as to whether the hospital had asked him to come back nearer harvest time, Shorty went on to say that since the illness he had taken a violent dislike to any food that was made from wheat or grain. The villagers, Maggie and I discovered, believed Shorty's story implicitly, and it was certainly true that Shorty was never seen to eat anything containing grain. He seemed to exist mainly on fruit and meat and didn't even eat bread. His aversion to grain didn't include drinks, however, since he was never known to be without a small flask of whisky in his inside pocket. No doubt the story had become distorted in the telling and retelling over the years before Maggie and I heard it, but we were both left with the impression that it did contain, dare I say? more than a grain of truth.

Shorty Smith had been working with horse manure all day long, and if he hadn't mentioned the fact, I think I would have guessed. He called to Maggie and me as we were walking by the river, and started asking me about opening a Post Office Savings Bank account. When we first started talking,

Shorty was upwind of me and the aroma was so overpowering that I discreetly changed positions, so that he was downwind. Shorty appeared not to notice, but as we talked he shuffled around until in a short while he had reversed our positions again. The smell really was unbearable. I stepped to one side and idly knocked a pebble into the water. When I stepped back I made sure that Shorty was downwind again. Shorty stopped, and absent mindedly plucked a stalk of grass, which he stuck between his teeth. The movement put him upwind once more, so after a few seconds I did the same to him.

As these manoeuvres continued I began to realize that we were covering quite a bit of ground. We were performing a sort of slow motion old-time waltz, and Maggie, who had seated herself in the grass at the water's edge, was now a small figure in the distance. Shorty and I concluded our business, and I returned along the bank to Maggie. I found her helpless with laughter, tears streaming down her face.

'Oh, you don't know how funny you looked,' she said. 'It was better than a Charlie Chaplin film.'

'Well,' I said, 'I couldn't bear that awful smell, but I couldn't very well tell Shorty that, could I.'

'I realize that,' said Maggie, 'but what you don't know is that some time ago Shorty told me that when he was talking to you he always arranged it so that he was standing upwind. He said that he simply couldn't bear the smell of that after shave that you use, and said that it made him feel quite sick.'

The litter that was left in the countryside was a constant problem to the farmers. Picnickers would leave broken bottles, on which animals could cut themselves, plastic bags which they could eat and so die, by the hundredweight. There was also now and again the odd item of old furniture, deliberately dumped. Young 'Enry seemed to suffer more than most, and Ben and Shorty were constantly being diverted from more important jobs to clear the litter and rubbish from some field. Matters came to a head one sunny spring-like afternoon when Young 'Enry and his employees saw a couple of cars drawn up on the verge near the small copse on Young 'Enry's farm. The nearby field, on which sheep were grazing, had been painstakingly cleared the day before, and now there was litter strewn around near the gate, and a family of four sitting on the grass, surrounded by bottles, flasks and biscuits.

Young 'Enry was livid, and so were his employees, but remembering some very nasty moments that he had lately had when remonstrating with litter louts, Young 'Enry swallowed his rage and went off across the fields to the farmhouse where his lunch was waiting. Ben and Shorty were not so tolerant. They objected to clearing up other people's rubbish, and decided to take revenge on the picnickers in their own way. They approached carefully, under cover of the hedge. Then they collected together as much litter as they could find without being seen by the unsuspecting visitors. Quietly opening the door of the little red mini they crammed it inside. The two soon got carried away with the task, pushing each other aside in their eagerness, and with stifled laughter they filled the car with bottles and cartons, paper and plastic. In their enthusiasm they also snatched up handfuls of leaves and twigs, and not a little good old-fashioned dirt. Into the car it all went. Ben was wheezing like a whale, and the usually morose Shorty was verging on hysteria. They were in the hedgerow in their search for rubbish, and when they found a heap of horse droppings, they threw that in for good measure, bending double in almost silent mirth.

By this time the seat were piled high with rubbish and they had some difficulty in closing the door.

'Here, hang on,' whispered Ben, and flung the last handful of horse manure inside. Then, with many a high-pitched giggle, they crept off in the direction of the farmhouse for lunch.

They were sitting in the doorway of the barn, their lunchpacks opened in their laps when they were approached by a gent in a smart suit, who was carrying a briefcase. He crouched in front of them, mopping his brow with a snow-white handkerchief, and eyed their drinks longingly as he spoke.

'I've walked all over this farm,' he said, 'I'm trying to find the farmer, can you please tell me where I'll find him?'

Ben and Shorty eyed the man with amusement. 'He's in the farmhouse having his dinner,' said Ben, spraying the man with crumbs.

'But I went there first of all,' said the man. 'That was hours ago, and the lady of the house sent me off to the copse by the main road. When I got there there was no one about except a party of picnickers, and I must have walked every field on this farm since then, looking for him. Are you quite sure that he's in the farmhouse now?'

'Certain,' said Ben, spraying jam tart. 'He's having his dinner.'

'Thank you,' said the man with a sigh. 'I'll walk back and bring my car round before I see him. I left it over on the main road by the copse.'

The man left and Ben and Shorty stood up and looked over the fields. The red mini was still parked there. The other car was gone. They watched the man's retreating figure for a moment in silence, their hilarity gone. Then without a word to each other they began to pack up their things.

'I think that we ought to find ourselves a job on the other side of the farm,' said Ben, thoughtfully.

'Yes,' said Shorty. 'One that'll keep us busy until tea time.'

In rural Norfolk, where the people are extremely independent to start with, problems and even danger can arise when they become elderly. The most independent man that we ever met was Charlie. Like his friends Ben and Percy, Charlie was a pensioner, and like the other two, he worked. He used to cut the grass for us and many other people in the village. He owned a machine that looked like the very first motor mower ever built, and it was always possible to find out where Charlie was working. You merely scanned the horizon for the clouds of smoke that the ancient machine emitted. Percy used to say that Charlie was the only man in

43

the country who could cut the grass and kill greenfly at the same time.

Charlie travelled from place to place on foot, pushing the infernal machine in front of him in a wheelbarrow. Once, after he had put in a very good afternoon's work in the garden and orchard, I offered to run Charlie and his machine up the road in the estate car, but I offered only once. Charlie looked at me with such an aggressive expression that I realized that I had made a mistake. He then told me that if I couldn't mind my own business I could find someone else to cut my grass. After that I always left him to get on with his work, but my conscience pricked me at times when I saw the old man struggling with the heavy machine, as I passed him in the comfort of the car.

It was Percy who first brought us the news of Charlie's accident. The evening before, Charlie had been mowing the grass in the churchyard. Percy had been cycling by and had stopped, as he said, 'For a bit of a mardle.' What had happened then was not too clear, but Charlie had somehow managed to get his foot under the rotating cutter. It had sliced off half his Wellington boot and all the toes from his right foot. Charlie had taken a length of string from his pocket and had tied it around and around his leg and boot in a series of clumsy tourniquets, and then, on Percy's old bike, had pedalled the seven and a half miles to the nearest hospital. When Maggie and I had demanded of Percy why the dickens he had allowed Charlie to do such a thing, he had looked hurt.

'He didn't stop to ask me,' he said, 'And I was too busy collecting up his toes from the cuttings to notice what he was up to.' Percy had followed Charlie to the hospital later, after he had found the missing toes, and had presented them in a jam jar to a surprised casualty nurse. 'They looked just like them adverts for king prawns in sauce,' he said.

Maggie and I visited Charlie that evening and took Percy along with us. I was rather sharp with the old man, and asked him why he hadn't called on us for help when the accident happened. I said that he knew that Maggie was a nurse, and that by car we would have got him to hospital and treatment in a matter of minutes.

The old boy shook his head stubbornly. 'You know it isn't my way to go around asking folk for help,' he said.

'Well hang it all Charlie,' I said. 'You took Percy's bike without even asking him for it. What's the difference? Isn't that accepting help?'

Charlie took a very deep breath. The stubborn look returned to his old face. 'The difference,' he said, 'is this. Percy had my mower as security against his bike, and my mower is worth a darn sight more than his old wreck.'

FOUR

MAY & JUNE

THE warmer days had arrived, and Maggie and I were kept busy in the garden, and doing the hundred and one repair jobs around the house that Maggie had been listing all through the winter months. After a dry spell that lasted for a couple of weeks or more, nature started redressing the balance with regular downpours of rain. We noticed that a damp patch appeared with each shower, in the corner of the ceiling in one of the bedrooms. I called in Whistling Jack to fix it.

Whistling Jack was a blue denimed, agile, bouncy young man who did most of the fixing in the village. Keen as mustard and as fit as a fiddle, he could be seen on any fine day working on some rooftop, and whistling. He didn't whistle a tune exactly, or if he did it was unrecognizable to anyone save himself, but he never, ever stopped.

On his first visit to the Post Office roof, Jack chose a fine dry morning and was up aloft before I had opened the shop. Around mid morning I stepped outside to see how things were going and was just in time to see Whistling Jack fall. The roof at the rear of the premises was quite an expanse of tiles, sloping from about forty five feet at the ridge to a mere six feet six at the eaves. With age the centre of this area had sagged somewhat leaving a shape rather like that of a ski jump. When I looked out, Jack was rolling down this slope like a large blue denimed football. At the eaves his trajectory was nearer the horizontal than the vertical, and he cleared the concrete path with ease, and bowled merrily across the lawn. I can't say for certain whether or not Jack was whistling on the way down, out of force of habit, but I wouldn't be surprised. Before I could inquire as to his condition, he picked himself up, shook himself like a terrier, and springing to the fourth rung of the ladder, whistled his way aloft again.

Indoors in the kitchen, I found Maggie sitting with her eyes closed and her fingers in her ears. The constant whistling was more than she could bear. I suggested that she might try diverting Jack for a minute or two by making him a cup of tea.

'I've tried that,' she wailed. 'He's drunk three cups already and there hasn't been a pause. I can't understand how he does it. He must have trained himself to whistle down his nose while drinking.'

I paid Jack later that day, and he left.

'Good job guv'er, no more trouble now, 'er,' and stuck for words, he whistled as he left.

The next time that we had a shower the damp patch reappeared. I sent for Whistling Jack again. As he started his merry work Maggie put on her coat.

'I'm going out until lunchtime at least,' she said. 'I'll leave you and Birdman together. I'll hide in the churchyard or something until he's gone.' She paused at the door. 'If he doesn't fix it this time,' she said, 'please don't tell him. I'd sooner have the damp patch any day than him.'

Later that day Whistling Jack left. Later that night the rains came. So did the damp patch.

It was a fine and sunny Wednesday half day, and for reasons that I cannot now recall, I decided to have a look at the roof myself. Getting from the ladder to the eaves was the hardest part of the job, and I was surprised, once up on the roof, to find how safe I felt. I found the cause of the leak within minutes. At the point where the chimney stack and the tiles met I found a tile dislodged. Its correct position could be easily seen as the whole of the roof that had been exposed to the elements had grown a colourful coating of lichen and moss. Pushing tentatively at the tile, I was rather

47

surprised when it clunked obligingly back into its original position. I took off one shoe, and gently tapped the lead flashing of the chimney down on to the tile. Then edging my way back down to the gutter, I yelled for Maggie to pass up the garden hosepipe so that I could test the repair. I soaked the tile and the surrounding area for over half an hour, and I couldn't make it leak. I jetted water at it from every angle, and with force, but I couldn't make the damp patch reappear in the bedroom. As I flung the hosepipe down on to the path I was feeling extremely pleased with myself. 'A good job well done,' I was saying, as I edged my way down the slope.

I think that the man who first said that pride goeth before a fall had probably had some dreadful experience of an ancient pantile roof! Although I had managed the descent to the eaves before without any difficulty, this time it was different. It was different because all the water that I had poured on to the repaired area had run down and turned the lichen and moss into a surface that was so slippery that it was impossible to stand on it, let alone walk. In an attempt to keep my balance I took a couple of hurried steps, arms flailing. The next moment I was completely out of control, running down the ski jump at an ever increasing speed. I realized pretty quickly that there was no possibility whatsoever of stopping when I reached the gutter. I was going to have to jump. As I neared the edge, the kitchen door opened and Maggie's head appeared below me. Vaguely recalling that men who drop things from a height for a living have some sort of warning that they shout, I racked my brains. I didn't have a great deal of time to spend on the subject. 'Look out below,' I gasped as I left the roof, and had a fleeting glimpse of Maggie's upturned astonished face as I became airborne, and sailed over her head like a deranged windmill, coming to earth with a thud and cartwheeling across the lawn.

It took me quite a few minutes to get my breath back and extract the rose branch that had got stuck up my right trouser leg. I was relieved to find that I was still in one piece.

'It would just serve you right,' said Maggie, 'if you had

broken something. Playing silly games at your age, you're just like a schoolboy.'

I protested, and started explaining that my death-defying leap had been one not of choice but of necessity, but Maggie cut me short.

'I don't believe you,' she said. 'As you jumped off the roof I distinctly heard you shout "Geronimo".'

The next day was Thursday, which was always a busy day in the shop. Apart from discovering a limp in my leg and a thorn in a very painful place, the morning passed uneventfully. Just before lunch who should stick his head through the door but Whistling Jack.

'Er, just been up on the roof Guv,' he said. 'Put it right for good this time. Old tile you know, porous. New one on now. Good job, er, no more trouble.'

'But wait a minute,' I said, but Jack carried on as if he hadn't heard me.

'No more to pay though,' he said. Then whistling loudly to signal the end of the conversation, he turned and bounced away.

Overnight we had the lightest possible shower of rain. The next morning the damp patch was back again.

A visitor to any of the flint cottages of the village would be almost certain to notice, fixed to a beam, or perhaps standing in a corner, a shotgun. Even old widows kept their husband's old guns, and the weapons were always within easy reach, in case a Sunday lunch should suddenly run across the lawn, or land in the orchard. Throughout the daytime and often in the night too, distant reports would go almost unnoticed, and should unexpected visitors call, hasty bartering with neighbours would always produce a brace of pheasants or a hare, or the very least a couple of pairs of pigeons. Shooting, then, in the village, was regarded as the most normal of pastimes, but when John took up shooting the whole village quaked. Cats were locked up in outhouses, dogs chained by the door, and a watch was kept on John's every movement by an anxious community. When Len had very wisely refused to sell one of his old guns to John, he had gone off in a huff and obtained what he said was a bargain from someone in the next village. It was a double barrelled twelve bore, with a loose stock and paper thin barrels. The ancient mechanism was so worn that the slightest vibration once the hammers were cocked would cause the gun to go off. As Ben said of it, 'If you loaded the blasted thing, stood it up in the corner and shouted "Fire" it would.'

Tales about John's hunting expeditions soon began to circulate. Miss Money, in a large feathered hat, had been mistaken for a pheasant by John on the other side of a hedge.

'You were lucky he was aiming straight at you,' said Percy, 'that way you were in no danger.'

The disappearance of a peacock from Lady Blanche's grounds was attributed to John's activities, and Len was heard to complain that it was people like John who got poachers a bad name with the police. A weathervane was shot to pieces on the roof of one of the farms, and the farmer swore that it had been done by John who had mistaken it in the dark for a flying goose. John denied this furiously and said that if anyone had a weathervane that was supposed to be an old man with a scythe, but looked like a flying goose, then it was a pretty poor thing in the first place and deserved to be shot down.

The day came when P.C. Danby called at Ben's cottage to see John and ask him if he had a licence for his shotgun. John foolishly replied that he didn't need a licence as he didn't own a gun. They were standing in the cottage kitchen, which was a lean-to extension to the main building, and as they talked the door of the broom cupboard in the corner swung open with a creak. John had hastily shoved the gun that he had been holding into the cupboard when he had seen Danby coming up the garden path. He should have ignored the swinging door, as the gun was well enough hidden behind a clump of brooms and brushes, but he didn't. He reached out a heavy hand and pushed the door to with a slam. Inside the cupboard, the old gun heard the slam, felt the vibration, and responded in its usual way. There was a deafening crash in

the tiny kitchen as both barrels went off at once, and the top
of the cupboard flew into a thousand tiny splinters. The ceiling above the cupboard disappeared in a cloud of plaster
dust, and a couple of tiles fell through the gap, through the
top of the cupboard, and into the brushes and brooms. The
door of the cupboard swung open again, and a half a dozen
brooms and mops fell out. The still smoking shotgun was
amongst them.

As the dust and silence settled together in the small room,
the body of a very small, very dead sparrow tumbled through

the hole in the tiles, through the cupboard top, and on to the pile of brooms.

P.C. Danby reached slowly into his left hand breast pocket and drew out his notebook with a sigh. 'It seems to me,' he said licking a fat finger and turning the pages of his book, 'that we've both made a small killing today.' He looked at the dead sparrow, and then he looked John slowly up and down. 'A very small killing,' he said.

As the days slipped by and the date of the village fete grew near, one member of the Village Hall committee suggested that as a change from Lady Blanche and the vicar, they should try to get some celebrity to open the proceedings. Funds wouldn't run to a nationally known television or film star but it was agreed that they should try to get someone who was well enough known to draw even bigger crowds to the fete than normal. Several minor celebrities were contacted, but as fees were quoted the committee's sights were lowered again and again, until they finally settled on a young lady from the city who had several second prizes in beauty contests, and earned her living as a model. Though disliked by the ladies on the committee, because of her reputation, she was popular with the men, mainly because of her outstanding bust measurement.

A letter was received from the young lady stating that due to unforeseen circumstances she would be travelling alone, and that she would expect, apart from her fee, transport to and from the nearest railway station, and a decent lunch. Miss Money was delegated to organize the lunch, and the men set about solving the transport problem. The hire of a car was out of the question, as the distance to be travelled was too great, and the car would be left standing for a couple of hours at least, until needed for the return journey. The men racked their brains. Percy had a car. He didn't use the old thing very often, but when it was out on the road it was an eye catcher. It was a nineteen thirty-six model and was now so old that it might be considered by some people to be respectable again, if only it was cleaned up a bit. It was

Young 'Enry who suggested that they should use the old car and pay Percy for the mileage. Cars of that age were all the rage in the city, he said. He had even seen some society female on the telly getting married and using a car that must have been every bit as old as Percy's. Ben said that the car on telly wouldn't have had mice in it like Percy's, but he was ignored by the rest of the committee, who saw a cheap way out of their difficulty. Percy was rather flattered by the suggestion, and agreed to the use of the car on the condition that no one else was allowed to drive it. It wasn't considered proper for Percy to travel alone on such an important mission, and competition for the other two seats in the vehicle was fierce. Whistling Jack said that it was obvious that he should go, as he was more important than most of the others, being the best bowler in the cricket team, and was also nearer to the lady's age than most. Hubby sneered at this and said that bowling had nothing to do with it. Wasn't he more famous for having grown a carrot in a drainpipe that turned out to be the biggest carrot ever seen in the village? Ben poured scorn on that idea, asking who the devil wanted to eat a great fat carrot that didn't taste of anything? In the end it was decided to draw lots for the privilege, and the winners were Whistling Jack and old Charlie.

When the great day came Percy refused to start the car until he had Whistling Jack's word that he would ride in the front seat on the return journey and leave Charlie in the back with the Beauty Queen. Jack agreed, but said with an injured air that he was mystified as to the reasoning behind such a request, and added that people shouldn't believe half of what they heard in the village pub.

The outward trip was uneventful and the young lady was greeted on time by Percy, face shining like a polished apple, trousers creased like razors. She smiled at Percy in a very sweet way, and even complimented him on his ancient motor, calling it 'A lavly old cor'. Her smile faded slightly when she saw the eager expression of Whistling Jack, and the pursed up attitude of his lips, due to all that whistling no doubt, made her ignore his outstretched hand. Her smile disappeared completely when she saw Charlie. He looked clean enough, in a homespun, threadbare kind of way, but he had misplaced his glasses, and his eyes were screwed up in his aggressive old face in a determined attempt not to miss any of the famous curves. It was by sheer accident that his eyes were directed to what was the young lady's most famous dimension, but she was not to know that, and she considered that stares of that kind, which she enjoyed when they came from virile young men-about-town, were positively indecent when they came from a man who was old enough to be her grandfather. She climbed into the rear seat, and after a slight pause, while Charlie and Percy each waited for the other to close the door, they moved off.

They were half-way back to the village, the Beauty Queen staring fixedly out of the side window and Charlie staring fixedly at the Beauty Queen, when the clutch started to slip. The car behaved like a drunken kangaroo. One minute they would be steaming steadily down the road, and the next they would be losing speed rapidly, while the engine raced. Then the clutch would snatch again and the car would leap forward, flinging the passengers about madly, only to slow down again after a few yards. The motion was made even worse by Percy's reactions, which were just a little bit behind events. When the car slowed down he would instinctively step on the accelerator, and when it suddenly picked up, he would brake, but by the time that he braked, the car itself was already slowing again. In the front seat Whistling Jack bounced around like a tennis ball. In the back, old Charlie and the Beauty Queen were thrown together in positions that were greatly appreciated by Charlie, but not at all by the young lady. She winced as the brim of his hat brushed against her expensive hair-do.

'Can't you take your hat off?' she shouted, over the engine's roar. Old Charlie complied eagerly, and loosened his collar and tie too with a fearsome smile.

When Percy at last decided that he would have to bring the old car to a halt for some mechanical adjustment to be made, he did so with such a sudden screeching of brakes that the two in the back were flung on to the cramped space of the floor in a tangled heap, old Charlie's face coming to rest crushed hard against the young lady's ample bosom. Asked later whether he had seen enough of the Beauty Queen, he answered that he hadn't, as he'd mislaid his specs, and that it had been like offering nut toffee to a man who had lost his false teeth.

When at last they arrived at the village hall it took the young lady longer to adjust her face than it had taken Whistling Jack to adjust the clutch, but the opening ceremony was performed on time. After the lunch, and a sympathetic half hour with Miss Money, the lady posed for a few photographs for the local paper. The fete was being held on the sports field and spilled over on to the children's playground. After being snapped pretending to throw a ball at the coconut shy, the Beauty Queen arranged herself on the children's see-saw for another picture. Percy, who was secretly nettled by Charlie's familiarity with the young lady, mounted the children's slide, and aimed a small camera down at her. He waited hopefully. The lady herself pretended not to notice his interest in her, but made a point of not walking under the slide while he was up there. She was standing at the bottom of the slide, talking to the photographer, when Percy in his eagerness leaned a little too far. He slipped and dropped the camera. Then he whizzed down the shute towards her on his stomach, the buttons on his waistcoat screeching as they slid. He struck the Beauty Queen at speed, and the two of them landed in a heap. The lady found herself in much the same position with Percy as she had been in with Charlie earlier in the day. She screamed, and beat Percy about the head with her fists, even continuing for a second or two after they had regained their feet.

She was livid. 'This blarsted village,' she yelled, the carefully controlled accent now gone, 'is full of nothing but geriatric sex maniacs.'

Percy drew himself up in what was for him a dignified

manner. He fingered one red ear gingerly as he spoke. 'You're wrong,' he said, 'we ain't all pensioners. The young uns will be along shortly, when they've finished work.'

The young lady refused to allow Percy to drive her back to the station, and Percy refused to allow anyone else to drive his car. Matters were at stalemate, until the arrival of our young village bobby on the scene. With his eyes nearly popping out of his head he said that as it was an emergency, and as he had nothing very important to do, he thought that it would be in order for him to run the lady to the station in his Panda car, all in the line of duty. The Beauty Queen forgot her outburst of temper, and regained the lost accent.

'You're an ebsolute dorling,' she beamed at him as he helped her into the car. Charlie and Percy watched the car disappear in the distance with mixed feelings, but the rest of the committee heaved a sigh of relief. It was possibly just as well that no sudden emergency arose during the rest of the day's proceedings, as the village bobby wasn't seen again for the rest of the day.

The fete drew crowds from miles around, and was acknowledged to be one of the finest village fetes in the area. The visitors would start arriving after lunch and by three o'clock the place would be as crowded as Royal Ascot. The fete was officially opened at one thirty but the crowd at that time consisted mainly of local people, and before the number of visitors grew, they took the opportunity of trying their hands at the stalls and sideshows. It was our first fete and Maggie and I trailed along behind Charlie, who together with Percy was doing the rounds. We knew that there was something in the wind concerning old Charlie, and we were interested to see the outcome.

Since his accident Charlie hadn't worked, and his friends were beginning to worry about him. The old boy had lost quite a bit of weight, and his eyesight was failing. He didn't visit the pub as often as he used to, and although he called in for his pension as regularly as ever, he spent very little on food, and nothing on tobacco. In the pub one night, during Charlie's absence, George had arranged a whip-round for the old man and everyone had given most generously, as he was well liked by all those who knew him well enough to see through the mask of aggression that he wore. Then George was faced with the problem of getting the independent old so-and-so to accept the money. After considerable thought and many impractical suggestions George said that he could fix it. He might have to make use of Charlie's failing eyesight, but it would be in a good cause. If Percy could persuade Charlie to go to the fete early, before the crowds, then the money would find its way into Charlie's pocket. 'And if you could sort of mislay his specs, it would help a lot,' said George.

The two old men were walking round the grounds, Percy as bright and cheery as ever. Charlie peering suspiciously at the stalls. They stopped first at the Tombola stand. Percy bought himself a ticket and when Charlie showed no signs of buying one, reached for his pocket and said, 'I'll have one for him as well.'

'That's a load of old squit,' said Charlie, 'I'll pay for my own.' And he did.

ALL NUMBERS ENDING IN A THREE WIN A PRIZE, said the notice. Percy drew ninety-nine, and lost. Charlie had a hundred and ten, and threw his ticket to the ground in disgust.

'Hang on,' said Young 'Enry, who was running the stall, 'hundred and ten wins the pound note.'

'Does it?' asked Charlie. 'It ain't on your blarsted notice board.'

'That's because there's only one pound note to be won,' said Young 'Enry. 'If I'd written it up I'd only have to rub it out again now wouldn't I?'

'You should have written it up anyway,' snapped Charlie. 'I might have been robbed.' He took the pound note sulkily. The next stop was the bowling alley that was being run by Ben.

'Come you on along,' he was shouting. 'Bowl fer a pig. Bowl fer a pig.'

The idea of the contest was to knock down as many of the numbered skittles as possible with three balls. The scores were noted, and at the end of the day the person with the highest score won a pig, or could take the cash equivalent instead. Percy went first, and although usually a pretty skilful bowler, managed to score only two, missing the skittles completely with two of the three balls. Charlie went next, and scored a moderate eight.

'Gaw,' whistled Ben in admiration, 'that'll take a bit o' beatin'.'

'What are you a-going on about?' demanded Charlie. 'Any fool can beat a score of eight, nine times out of ten.'

'I don't know about that,' said Ben. 'They never run true on a hot day like today. Look what happened to Percy here.'

'Squit,' said Charlie. 'A score of eight ain't worth two-pence.'

'Oh yes it is,' said Ben. 'In fact it's worth a sight more than that. I'll give you a pound note for it if you want to sell your chance of winning.'

'Done,' said Charlie, and took his pound.

George was running the coconut shy, and I could see at once why he had visited the store earlier that morning and bought a length of fine fishing line. Charlie rubbed his eyes and peered at the target. He took careful aim at the middle one of three coconuts and let fly. His ball struck the left hand nut a glancing blow. Immediately the right hand nut leapt into the air and fell to earth with a thud.

'Ricochet,' said George. 'Darn good shot.'

The second ball missed completely, but the third one seemed to draw a coconut from its seating by the rush of air as it sped by. Old Charlie was so bucked by his performance that he decided to have another go. Again he did well, and went on, riding his winning streak. Eventually George congratulated him, and explained that he had now won six coconuts. George's total stock. Would Charlie be a pal and accept a pound note instead of the coconuts? Charlie wouldn't. But he would accept two pounds.

By now Charlie was feeling so intoxicated with success that he was prepared to have a go at anything. He peered short-sightedly at the darts stall, but Percy had to lead him away when the lady in charge panicked and started to scream. Charlie then turned his attention to the try-your-strength machine. He swung the giant mallet with such vigour that he lifted himself of his feet and sunk the mallet deep into the turf. Whistling Jack, who was waiting with his catapult, missed with his first shot, and Charlie was up on his feet again before the bell gave out a feeble ping.

'Almost miraculous,' said the vicar, who was in charge, standing in for Shorty Smith who had left on the pretext of helping out in the beer tent. The vicar handed Charlie a pound note and the old man said that he would have another go, but Percy grabbed his arm and led him away, as they were getting some very nasty looks from a burly stranger who had almost lifted the bell from its mountings and had been rewarded with a plastic whistle.

The loudspeakers crackled, and Miss Money's voice came over the air. Programme number so-and-so had won the draw, and would the lucky owner go and collect the pound note.

'That's your number,' said Percy.

'I ain't even got a programme,' said Charlie.

'Course you have,' said Percy. 'I got us one each, and don't think I've forgotten that you still owe me a shilling for yours.' Charlie paid his shilling, and then collected his pound.

He was now convinced that he had acquired the Midas touch. He even patronized the Women's Institute stall, where a large fat lady was inviting people to guess the weight of a large fruit cake. Charlie screwed up his eyes and squinted at the cake and then named a figure that must have been at least half a stone out. Then he hung around for half an hour, with an anticipatory smile on his face, until the fat lady called him a dirty old man, and asked him who he thought he was leering at.

At last, when the sports field was becoming congested, and the car park jammed with visitors' cars, Percy managed to drag Charlie away. As they went they passed the beer tent, where George's wife was doing a roaring trade in bottled beer. Feeling strangely wealthy, Charlie marched in, followed by Percy, and ordered two bottles of ale. When they were placed before him and the price stated, he stiffened.

'Why that's two pence more than they are in the pub,' he protested.

'Well, of course,' said the landlady, 'but even so, it's a sight cheaper than the prices that are charged in beer tents at other village fetes.'

'Well I think you've got a blarsted nerve,' said Charlie. 'You can keep 'em, and you can tell George from me that I don't come to the rotten fete just to get robbed.'

The annual sports day was held on the playing field on the second Wednesday after the village fete. It was, as all the sports days that I can remember from my own childhood were, a trial to teachers and parents, and a bore to most of the children. The children sat in restless ranks on the grass while their teachers, flustered and self conscious, tried vainly to keep to a timetable that had been printed long before it was known that little Jimmy Bloggs had got himself locked in the toilet, or that Harry Higgins had fallen into the river and had gone off home to change. When at last some team of runners patterned flat-footedly along the slippery grass track, everyone clapped and cheered just for something to do. Out of the many fidgety mothers and few bored stiff fathers who attended the sports day, it would have been very difficult indeed to find anyone who had really enjoyed themselves.

The winners received certificates, which the parents were disappointed with, and the children unimpressed by, and boys who could and did run like the wind when going about their own business were placed third and fourth behind boys whose parents had promised them a new something or other if they did well. It seemed a very long afternoon.

The village schoolmistress, who had spent more time and energy on the event than was required to organize the Olympic Games, was in a flap. The runners for the next race were nowhere in sight. They were somewhere among the small figures that were spread out all over the outfield. In the distance small groups of them could be seen, oblivious of time, wandering, chasing butterflies, throwing stones into the river, or wrestling on the grass. After repeated calls over the loudspeaker system, which was always left up for the occasion after its use on fete day, Miss Money took the microphone from the schoolmistress. Using her best Sunday School voice, she spoke.

'Now pay attention all you children,' she crackled over the air. 'This is most important.' Then seeing the figures in the distance who were paying not the slightest attention to her, 'If any of you can't hear what I'm saying, please raise your right hand.' A feeble titter came from the crowd at this, then it settled back into its bored stupor. But something did happen to brighten up the day, and it gave the village something to talk about for weeks after.

The village menfolk had quite a store of yarns concerning the sea and boats. They all spoke knowingly of steam drifters that used to work out of Yarmouth in the old days, of wherries that used to sail the broads, and of all night sea angling expeditions off Cromer and other places on the coast.

When Ben and his son John appeared on the field as the sports were ending and offered to take some of the members of the bored visiting families on a river trip, the good people placed their lives in the intrepid sailors' hands without a second thought. It might have been the seamen's jerseys that fooled them, or perhaps they had heard some of the yarns. When they saw the boat, the visitors hesitated for a second, but having already placed their money in John's outstretched palm, they climbed aboard.

The boat had been borrowed from Len, who was under the impression that the two were going on an afternoon's fishing. It was a woodworm riddled, flat bottomed punt, a craft that had been designed to float lightly and silently through shallow waters, in the pursuit of wildfowl. The courageous travellers, a tall knobbly man with bright ginger hair, three children of various sizes, each one a small reproduction of himself, and his wife, a small mousy woman, took up most of the punt, and Ben, crouching in the stern, looked at the level of the water apprehensively. Then he looked at John, the heavier member of the crew.

'Walk along the bank,' he called to his son. 'I'll take her down and you can bring her back.'

John didn't much fancy the idea of walking, but he could see his father's point. He unhitched the rope that tethered the punt, and gripping one end of it, followed the boat at a gentle walk as it drifted into midstream. He was just thinking to himself what a very pleasant way to make money this was, almost like being paid for taking your dog for a walk, when the rope jerked gently in his hands. The punt was in the current, and was picking up speed. John increased his pace to a fast walk. It was about then that he noticed that the pole was missing from the punt, and he remembered that Len had said that they would have to collect it from his cottage, as he never left it in the boat, lest someone should take a liking to it. The river was a very small and shallow one, not much more than a stream really, but it took hold of the punt gleefully, and carried it along. They came to the first of many bends, and the curve was in the river's favour, and not John's. He was forced to run round the outside of the curve, and to cover twice as much distance as the punt, just to remain level. The rope, which was not much more than twelve feet long, was tugging him towards the water's edge as the boat gained speed. John pounded round the bend. The boat was now definitely towing him, and his short thick legs were having some difficulty making the pace. He leaned away from the water, at an ever increasing angle, and as his speed increased, so did his feeling of panic. A tree loomed up in between him and the water. With a strangled gasp he charged at the narrow gap between the tree and the water. His lowered head snapped off a shower of twigs as he hounded through, and it was only his incredible speed that prevented him from losing his balance and falling into the river. After that John was running absolutely flat out. He thundered along the bank, his legs working like pistons.

It was fortunate for the coypus that had burrowed away at the bank that they were not at home when John dropped in. Ben, in the punt, had watched with mounting alarm as his son had steadily lost control of the situation. Then John had disappeared before his eyes, leaving the rope trailing in the water.

'John,' yelled Ben, his voice high with panic. 'What the hell are you a-doing?'

He was answered with a groan, and John's muddy head appeared over the bank and grew smaller as the punt sped on its way. Ben applied himself to the task of slowing the punt down. The only oar that he could find in the boat was a short double-ended thing that had started its life in a canoe. Old Ben grabbed the thing and dug it savagely into the water. The punt swerved and headed straight for the bank. The little mousy woman screamed, and as if at a prearranged signal, the three children all started to cry together, very loudly. Ben applied the paddle again, this time at the other side of the punt. The craft spun completely round, rapidly, and with a sickening motion. Then it continued on its way, as quickly as before, but sideways. The big ginger man leaned towards Ben.

'The kids are feeling sick,' he said, in a slow loud voice. 'Stop the boat.'

In desperation Ben tried dipping the paddle first at one side, then the other. To do this in a broad flat punt meant that he had to cause a certain amount of rocking motion. The punt zig-zagged crazily for a while and then spun completely round again. The little woman screamed at the top of her voice. One child was sick in the bottom of the boat, and the other two sobbed in terror.

'Stop it,' roared the big ginger man. He shouted this at Ben and not at his family. Ben flung down the paddle in despair, but not before he had noticed that they were now travelling backwards.

John appeared again, this time ahead of them. He had cut across the fields while the punt was winding its erratic way around the bends, and he was now in a position to offer some assistance to his despairing parent, if only he could think what form the assistance should take. He couldn't, and he and Ben stared into each other's face in silent impotence as the punt slid swiftly by.

Ben was now both angry and frightened. 'Do something can't you,' he screamed at his son. 'I knew I should never have let you talk me into this.'

The big ginger man clenched his fists. 'Do you mean to say that you've never done this before?' he shouted. He started to stand up.

It was then that the punt tipped over. It didn't turn over, but with the three children all draped over one side, being sick, and the big ginger man leaping to his feet, it tipped far enough over for all the occupants to be thrown out, and then it righted itself again. The water was only about eighteen inches deep at that point, and the current was not strong enough to impede them as they waded ashore, gripping one dripping child each. The empty punt sailed merrily on its way.

Hours later, scrubbed and dried and strangely subdued, Ben and John sat in two fireside chairs, in silence. They had had to pay for a taxi to take the ginger family home, and they had been assured by the big ginger man that they would hear from him soon, as soon, he said, as he could get a doctor to check on the health of his ginger family. The day had been an extremely unprofitable one, and the two sat with their bedtime drinks before them untouched, each with his own thoughts. There came an angry pounding on the front door, and then it burst open as the caller lost patience. An irate figure stamped into the room. It was Len, and he wanted to know where the devil his punt was.

The warm dry weather at the end of June had encouraged Maggie and me in our new-found hobby of walking. We met many people who we would never have met otherwise, and although our walking had to take place before breakfast or after tea, we were always surprised at the number of other people who were to be met, also walking. Many people had no other means of transport of course, and this meant that age-old footpaths were in regular use, although during the month of July some difficulty concerning one footpath led to a very interesting confrontation.

FIVE

JULY & AUGUST

THE countryside around the villages was interwoven with footpaths. In our rambles, particularly in the summer months, Maggie and I covered mile after mile, following the paths through farmyards and fields, through orchards and smallholdings, and never once were we prevented from passing. The landowner or tenant would mostly wave to us, or sometimes stop and have a word or two, and each meeting was as friendly as possible.

When the solicitor from the city bought the White Bungalow, the footpath that ran across the meadow in front of the bungalow was in constant use. Children from the other end of the village used it to get to school, and their mothers used it to get to the church and the Post Office. The menfolk rarely had cause to use the path, but they were as incensed as the women and children when the new owner tried to dissuade one and all from using the footpath. On the first occasion the children had reported to their parents that there was a large bull loose in the field. They were all so much afraid of the bull that they had taken the longer route to school and had all been late. When their fathers investigated they found an animal that was somewhere in between a large calf and a small bull in its state of growth. It was certainly loose in the meadow, and was a frisky animal, running towards the men with tossing head, and snorting. The men dismissed it with a slap and a shout, but the children would understandably have run. A deputation of the village menfolk went to see the solicitor, and politely pointed out that the animal was interfering with the villagers' wishes to use the public right of way, and was causing a deal of inconvenience. The newcomer stated loftily that he was a very busy man indeed, and didn't have time to waste on trivialities. He was breaking no law that he knew of, there was no case for him to answer, and would they please leave. Unused to such unco-operative attitudes, the men left, and as they did so their feeling towards the newcomer were expressed openly.

As the calf grew bigger, and became indisputably a bull, the villagers thought that they now had grounds for action, but the solicitor was ahead of them. The bull was removed, and replaced by a large and savage looking dog. Even the menfolk didn't like the look of the dog, and more than one person was heard to say that he would shoot the animal and take the consequences, but nothing was done. The man was, after all, a solicitor, and in any case, one fierce dog could easily be replaced by another. The deputation called at White Bungalow again, and this time they were in a different mood. They demanded that the dog be removed at once. The solicitor told them that as the dog hadn't bitten anyone yet, it couldn't be called a savage or dangerous dog. He added that if they thought that they had a case, they could always take him to court. Charlie and Ben, who had gone out of curiosity, took a hearty dislike to the man, and although they never had cause to use the footpath themselves, they decided to help those who did. Over their beer they hatched a plot to take the newcomer down a peg or two.

It was Sunday evening, and the drive of White Bungalow was packed with cars. The solicitor and his wife were entertaining. In the lounge, one of the guests, a barrister, was standing with his wife looking out of the window that overlooked the meadow. A five foot wattle fence separated the garden from the field, and beyond it could be seen the gently rising grassland, with beech trees on the horizon.

'All very pleasant, my dear,' said the barrister to his wife, as he sipped from his wineglass. 'All very peaceful and rural, and – Good Heavens!' Across their field of vision there had floated a figure. A figure that had an unwashed unshaven face, and wearing an idiotic leer. The gaping mouth disclosed one yellow tooth, and on the creature's head there was a dirty battered old hat with a turned down brim. As it slowly floated past, shielded from the waist down by the wattle fence, the figure leered into the guests' faces.

'Eek,' said the barrister's wife.

'Ah,' said the barrister, and the sounds brought the solicitor hurrying to the window. By the time he got outside and on to the footpath, the figure was away across the meadow in the distance. As it reached the stile, it dismounted from the old penny farthing bicycle that it was riding, one that was usually only seen on fete days and special occasions, and lifted it over the stile. The large savage dog was lying in the grass, chewing contentedly on what could easily have been part of an elephant.

Back in the dining-room, the soup had just been served when another 'Eeek' from the barrister's wife caused the guests to look towards the window again. The figure was floating by again, slowly. It was in fact moving so slowly that its speed must have dropped almost to stalling point. Again, it leered. It leered so evilly that one of the other guests dropped her soup spoon with a clatter. The figure glided silently on its way, and out of view. The now enraged solicitor shot from the dining-room into the kitchen, through the back door and along the garden path, through the door in the fence and on to the footpath. By the time that he got there the figure was quite a distance away, and going at a pretty smart pace. The savage dog was snoring contentedly, its head resting on a giant sized bone.

It was as the company were settling down to a game of bridge that the early warning 'Eek' was heard again. All heads turned towards the windows. The apparition that floated past was a different one, but none the less objectionable as far as the guests were concerned. This figure had a shining bald head and thick round spectacles. Its bitter old face wore a defiant expression, and as it passed, it didn't smile or leer as the other figure had done, but stared aggressively at the guests as if defying them to do something. So stern was its visage that the barrister's wife let out another involuntary 'Eeek' as their eyes met.

It was perhaps no more than twenty minutes later that the next 'Eeek' was heard. This time it was uttered by one of the other ladies whose nerves were not quite up to such happenings, and in any case, had always tried to keep abreast of current fashion.

'Eeek,' she squeaked.

'Oh, eeek,' answered the barrister's wife.

Along the fence an army of ragged urchins had appeared, visible from the waist up. They bobbed along with a jerky, unnatural kind of motion, like a lot of marionettes on the ends of invisible strings. There were dark children and fair children and ginger children. There were children with freckled noses, children with snub noses, and children with runny noses. There were children with black eyes, children with cross eyes, some with buck teeth, and some with no teeth. And as they silently wobbled past, they each stared solemnly in at the guests with mutely accusing eyes.

The guests had departed early, and the solicitor, after going outside and kicking the large savage dog, which had shown the first signs of life for a couple of hours by biting him, had called in at the village pub to have a word with the locals. Ben and Charlie he immediately recognized as the two penny farthing cyclists. Choosing his words with extreme care, he addressed himself to them. In conciliatory tones he explained that although he was the most reasonable of men, and could enjoy a joke as much as the next man, he really couldn't allow a repeat performance of the kind of evening that he had just experienced. Charlie glowered at him in silence, but Ben answered in a deceptively friendly tone.

'No law has been broken, it's a public right o' way,' he said. 'If you think you've got some kind o' case, you could always go to court.' He took a slow pull at his pint before he went on. 'O' course, if you did take somebody to court, and if you was lucky enough to win, I'd bet that somebody else would go and do the same sort o' thing, and you'd be right back where you started.'

The solicitor gripped his glass tightly, and remained in silent thought for a minute or two. 'Those children,' he said, with a pleading note in his voice, 'what were they doing?'

'Why, trying out our idea,' said Ben. 'They were so scared of going by your dog that we knocked em up a pair o' stilts each, to go to school on. They're going to use them all the time from now on.' He grinned. 'At least as long as there's a great dog in the meadow that might rush out and bite 'em.'

The solicitor was silent for another long minute, and then he spoke. 'I think,' he said, 'that in the interests of harmony, it might be as well if I kept the dog on the other side of the fence. I mean in my garden, and not in my meadow.' He emphasized the word MY. 'I think that I'll try it for a while at least, as a sort of experiment.'

'Now that's a very good idea,' said Ben, as though the thought had never occurred to him. 'But if I were you I would keep the old dog in there permanent like, and never let him out again. Some people are apt to go up in the air over a little thing like that, you know.'

One sunny summer Sunday Maggie and I shut up the shop and headed for the coast. We were only a few miles from our destination, driving down a tree-lined road, when we passed a sign that said DEER! I lifted my foot and let the car slow down to thirty-five. As I did so, the car behind, which had been trailing us closely for a couple of miles, pulled out and passed us with a roar. Ahead, two graceful forms leapt from the bank and into the road. The leader, a handsome stag, reached the other bank in three graceful bounds. The second animal, a young doe, had only reached the crown of the road when the accelerating car struck it. I stopped the car before we got to the deer, and Maggie and I both got out. The deer's enormous liquid eyes were already glazing over when we got to her, and within a few seconds a great gout of blood from her dainty nostrils and mouth announced her death. We dragged the limp, warm body to the verge, gripping the small cloven hooves, and as we did so we noticed another injury on one hind leg. Dried blood. Not a fresh wound. Not a wound that would kill an animal. Just one that might slow it down a little.

Our mood was changed by the incident. We spoke not a single word to the driver of the car that had struck the deer, but left him standing at the roadside. Perhaps it was best to leave his conscience to criticise. Instead of continuing to the coast, we decided to have a ploughman's lunch at the next pub that we came across, and then turn back for home.

As we nibbled at our food in silence we couldn't help overhearing the conversation of the only two other customers in the bar. They were two men in tweed jackets, and they were talking, in between mouthfuls of bread and cheese and beer.

'Nearly had one o' your blarsted animals yesterday, Fred,' said one of them. 'Them young uns can clear the fence in places you know, specially this time o' year.'

'You wouldn't shoot it just for a bit of trespassing, would you?' asked the other.

'No,' said his friend, 'any case, I only had a rabbiting gun with me at the time, not much good for deer. A young doe she were, and bor, were she quick. Still, I stung her backside for her. That'll teach her to keep to your side of the fence.'

The two men carried on with their eating and talking. We left, still in silence, and drove slowly back down the tree-lined road. When we passed again the spot with the dark stain on the tarmac, Maggie borrowed my handkerchief.

It was during the hot days of July and August that I first met the village blacksmith. The smithy had been closed for some time when we moved into the village. The old anvil and bellows had been removed, and the premises were used as garage space. The retired smith was still living in the village, and meeting him was something of a surprise. Instead of the robust giant of man with large sinewy hands that one expects a smith to be, he had the appearance of an emaciated jockey. He was well into his seventies, but it was obvious that even in his heyday he had been a bit of stripling. I mentioned this to Percy one day and asked him if the man had been a very good blacksmith. Percy had answered that 'At that time o' day, and when you were built like him, you had to be a darn sight better than good, to make your living as a smith.'

When the town water was first piped to the village the authorities met with considerable opposition from some of the old folk. Many of them refused point blank to use the town water, preferring their old pumps. As time went by, they had all capitulated one by one, and the old wells had fallen into disuse, and the last and only one who was still using his own well water was the old smith. Samples of the water had been taken, and condemned as unfit to drink, but the old man was stubborn.

'I've drunk this well water since the day I was born,' he said, 'and I'll drink it until the day I die.'

I tried to reason with him once, sitting by the well on a sunny afternoon, but every argument that I put up in favour of the town water was met by one in favour of the old well. I reminded the old boy of the increase in the use of chemicals on the land, and suggested that a fair amount of these might find their way into the water that he drew from the well. The old smith agreed, but said that the town water was full of chemicals anyway. I said that I had looked down his well, and found it full of beetles and other forms of animal life.

'So it is,' he answered, 'but they're all at the top, and I draw my water from the bottom.'

I gave up eventually, and as I left, I thought to myself that the man would never drink town water as long as he lived. But he did, although the old smith himself never knew it.

The smith's wife was built more like a blacksmith than he was. She would have been exceptionally tall and broad if she had been a man. As a woman, she was huge. It was odd to think that the frail old blacksmith would fill a bucket with coal, and then would have to call his wife to carry it indoors. When the smith was taken ill, and took to his bed, his wife had to do all the fetching and carrying, and that included drawing water from the old well in the garden. Every time that she went outside with the water bucket she had to pass through the kitchen, where the new water tap sat, unused. The temptation eventually became irresistible, and she

72

started using the tap water. The old smith never noticed. His illness had blunted his sense of taste, and he didn't drink plain water by itself. He assumed that the tea and soup that his wife was giving him was being made in the same old way, with the well water. He remained bedfast for weeks, and the village began to think he would never recover, but he did. When Dr John told him that he was well enough to put on his clothes and go downstairs for a while, he took this to be a sign that he had completely recovered, and once downstairs, stepped out into the garden for a breath of air. His wife left him there, sitting in the shade for a couple of hours, and when she returned, the old man complained that he didn't feel too well, felt rather sick.

'You've probably overdone things, this being your first day up,' she soothed him, and helped him back up to bed. The next day the old smith felt worse, and the day after that the doctor had to be called in a hurry.

The old man was rushed to hospital, and was found to be very ill indeed. When the life finally went out of his tiny weakened frame, gastro-enteritis was given as the cause of his death. When he had been admitted, the doctor had asked the smith's wife whether he had eaten anything unusual in the past few days.

'No,' she answered, 'only biscuits and soup.'

But as his widow, she guessed what had happened, and it was while Maggie was comforting her after the funeral that she shared her secret with her. The day after the old smith had been taken into hospital she had found his mug on the seat by the well. It still contained a drop of well water, which didn't smell very nice. She had taken the cover from the well, and looked down. The water, condemned as unfit so long ago, had not improved by remaining unused for week after hot week. Floating in the water there was the bloated body of a dead rat. As the old smith himself said, he drank the well water from the day he was born, and he drank it until he died.

Maggie had caught the home made wine craze from the

other women in the village, and was filtering and bottling, surrounded by jars and tubes and vinegar flies when I broke the news to her about the bantams.

'The bantams are dead,' I said.

We had these attractive little birds for several weeks, and had grown extremely fond of them. They provided us with four or five eggs every day, and were cheap to feed, eating up all the kitchen scraps. But they were more than merely a source of fresh eggs. They had become like pets to us, and Maggie could call each one by name and it would come to her.

I had gone to put them to bed for the night, to shoo them into the hut and close the pop hole behind them. Instead of being greeted by the usual clucking and scratching, I had found them all stretched out in the run, in the most un-natural positions, and already growing cold. I brought the body of the colourful cockerel into the kitchen, and we ex-amined it. When I held the bird in one hand, its head dropped right over in a position that would surely have been painfully impossible had the bird been alive. Did this mean that its neck had been broken? As all the other bantams were found to be in the same state, we hardly thought so, unless some animal had chased them around the run until they had broken their own necks. If that had been the case, wouldn't the animal have eaten at least one of them? Or at least bitten it? There wasn't a mark that we could see on any of the bodies, and in the end we decided that they must have been poisoned in some way. I heaped the bodies up in the corner of the hut, and promised to get up an hour earlier the next day so that I could bury them before Maggie came down. She was too upset to wish to witness their mass funeral, and I also felt very bad indeed about the whole business.

At the crack of dawn the peace of the countryside was shattered by a deafening chorus of shrieks and screams. Maggie and I both leapt out of bed and dashed out to the henhouse, where the noise seemed to be coming from. The corpses of the bantams had come to life. They were staggering around the run, falling over each other, or just leaning

74

against the wire in a state of complete exhaustion. Instead of a series of contented clucks they were emiting hoarse shrieks that made them sound more like peacocks than bantams. Every now and then, one of them would lunge towards the now empty water bowl in rage, and then would stagger off shrieking again. I ran and grabbed a pailful of water, which they soaked up as if they were a pack of camels that had just crossed the Sahara. Maggie was watching them in stunned disbelief, and kept shaking her head. 'It's the rice. It's the rice,' she kept muttering.

'What on earth are you talking about?' I demanded.

She explained. She had made a new type of wine, based on rice and raisins, from a recipe that had been given to her by one of the other wine makers in the village. After making the wine, she had scattered the used rice and raisins in the run, as a treat for the birds.

'They seemed to enjoy it so much,' she said.

'Of course they enjoyed it,' I said, 'they've probably never been on a binge before. They were dead last night all right, dead drunk.'

We found out later, after the news had sped round the village about the hen party at the Post Office, that the rice and raisins were intended to make a second batch of wine after the first, and after that, they would only be fit to give to the birds after they had been soaked in water for twenty-four hours or so. The story caused a great deal of amusement, but one or two customers asked us quite seriously if we would sell them any eggs that we got from the birds that day. They seemed to assume that they would have a very special flavour but when Maggie and I tried them we were disappointed, finding them quite normal.

By lunchtime the bantams appeared to have recovered, except for their exceptional thirst. The little cockerel, who must have had the largest share of the alcoholic food, as he did everything else, kept practising his crowing. He couldn't manage his normal 'Cock-a-doodle-doo' and as he strained away the harsh shrieking that he did produce sounded to us strangely like 'Never again, never again.'

When Granny Coster got herself a puppy, it was dying. The little Jack Russell terrier was wasting away with some bowel disorder, and its owner was about to have it destroyed, lest it should infect the rest of the litter. Granny Coster took it in and mothered it. She treated it exactly as she would have treated a child that had the same symptoms, and she had had considerable experience in that direction. She crammed the pup with herbal remedies and oatmeal, with hard boiled eggs and arrowroot, and as much liquid as she could force into it. The little dog lived, and grew to be as healthy as any of its brothers and sisters.

Granny also had a couple of cats. These animals, like many cats in the village, spent much of their time on the cottage roof. It was quite a common sight in the summer months to see a cat dosing on the ridge tiles, or leaning against a warm chimney. The fact that most of the old cottages were not much more than six feet high at the eaves made access to the roof an easy matter, and the presence of a cat on the roof made the sparrows think twice about nesting in the gutters.

When Granny Coster's dog grew big enough to chase the cats, it soon learnt to follow them on to the roof. It would reach the tiles in two leaps, one on to the rainwater butt, and the next on to the roof. In time the cats vacated the rooftop and the little dog took over. It spent long hours up there, and returned to earth only when Granny called it for its food, or when visitors arrived. The two cats found themselves a comfortable spot in the oven. It was a large cast iron oven at the side of the open fire, and every day, except for once a fortnight when Granny baked, the cats would creep inside and sleep the day away, their fur smelling in the heat.

One day a knocker was working his way through the village. A knocker is a man who knocks at the door, especially the doors of elderly people, and tries to buy antiques or curios that the householder might possess. Since experience had taught the villagers that many of the knockers were out to rob people if they could, they were treated accordingly. When the knocker called on Granny Coster, she got rid of him by pretending to be deranged, a ploy that she had used successfully before. The man pointed past her, to a small table, and offered her five pounds for it. Granny looked at him with a smile and asked him 'When did this happen?' The man pointed out a small brass wall plaque, and asked if Granny wished to sell it.

The old lady stared up at the sky and said, 'Last Tuesday, I should think.' After a few exchanges like this, the knocker had had enough. As he turned away, with a shake of his head, he muttered, 'Bats in the ruddy belfry.'

Behind him, Granny cackled with laughter. 'Oh no I ain't,' she called. 'Oh no I ain't. But I've got cats in the oven and a dog on the roof.' The man hurried away.

One character who I would dearly like to meet again, is Clocky Davis. Clocky used to travel around the village, offering to mend watches and clocks, or to buy any old broken movements that were beyond repair. I had been clearing out some drawers and had collected four or five old watches together. None of them had been worth very much, even when new, and I had discarded each one at one time or another as not being worth the cost of repair. I had been about to throw the lot into the dustbin when Maggie had mentioned that she had heard that Clocky Davis was in the village, and that he might give me a pound or two for them, so I held on to them.

It was raining cats and dogs when Clocky arrived, and he looked such a picture of abject misery as he stood dripping and shivering in the Post Office that I gave him the old watches for nothing. From the surprise that he showed, it was obvious that he wasn't used to getting anything for nothing, and he thanked me profusely before he left.

He was back again early the next day, and he showed me one of the watches that I had given him. I remembered it well. It had been discarded by me because of a habit that it had of stopping at around ten minutes to four. It would go all right for a day, perhaps one, two or three, but eventually it would stop, and always around ten to four. I explained this to Clocky.

'Ah, yes,' he said, 'but I don't think you realize just what a good watch you've given me, that's why I've brought it back.' He went on and explained using a great number of technical terms, that he had found such and such a fault in such and such a part, and this would indeed cause the watch to stop, and always in the same place. As it was such a very good watch in all other respects, he thought that it should be repaired. The parts would cost four pounds, and the labour he would throw in for nothing. ' 'Cos you've bin such a gent.'

I agreed to have the watch mended. After all, four pounds wasn't very much to pay for a good timekeeper. The next morning Clocky was back again bright and early. The watch was ticking away merrily. I thanked him for all his trouble, and paid him his four pounds. Then he disappeared. Thinking about him later, I realized that Clocky always disappeared. No one in the village knew exactly where he came from, or just when he would call again. He simply appeared and disappeared whenever he felt like it. Then I thought about the watch, and a vague suspicion crossed my mind. I dismissed it quickly. 'No,' I told myself, 'it isn't possible. No one but a complete idiot would give someone a watch because it was broken, and then buy it back from them in the same unbroken state, for four pounds. I mean to say, they just wouldn't do it, would they?'

I drove the thought from my mind, but found myself keeping an anxious eye on the watch. It kept excellent time for three whole days. On the fourth day it stopped. At ten minutes to four.

Tom Pearson had a smallholding in between our village and the next one. Tom grew fruit and vegetables, raised a few pigs, and was almost self supporting. He lived in a world of his own, and had long ago decided that putting his clocks backwards and forwards every year was a waste of time, and the clocks in his house were never altered, so that he was at least one hour out of step with the rest of the country for a good part of each year. After a while he grew so used to ignoring the time that other people went by that when his watches lost or gained he was quite unaware of it. He rose in the mornings and went to bed in the evenings with the birds, and claimed that he was healthier for it.

When Clocky Davis had been making his rounds, the day before he called at the Post Office, one very old grandfather clock in Tom Pearson's house had stopped, and Tom missed the loud ticking of the thing. He called Clocky in to have a look at it, and then left him alone in the house while he went to tend to his pigs. Clocky soon got the old clock going, and then sought out Tom in the piggery and got his pay.

When Tom returned to the house later, he found that the clock was working all right, but that Clocky, unaware of Tom's eccentricity, had set the grandfather to the time that his own pocket watch had shown. Then, thinking that he was doing Tom a favour, he had set all the other clocks in the house to the correct time. Tom was incensed. He chased around the village until he found Clocky, who was sitting on a grass verge, surrounded by curious children, and was stuffing an ancient wall clock into an equally ancient suitcase.

'What have you done to all my clocks?' Tom demanded. 'How the devil can I tell the right time now, when there ain't one of them that's right?'

'What are you talking about?' asked Clocky. 'They all tell the right time. I set 'em by my own watch, what more do you want?'

'I want my clocks to tell me my time, not yours,' said Tom, dancing with rage.

'What are you going on about?' demanded Clocky. 'Why should you have your own time and be different to everybody else?'

'Because I've always lived by my time, and I'm going to die by my time, and not yours or anyone elses,' shouted Tom.

'You're off your head,' said Clocky, 'but I'll tell you what to do. Go back home and stop every blarsted clock in the house. Then according to your reckoning, you'll live forever.'

Tom realized that all the talking in the world wasn't going to get Clocky to return to his house and readjust all the clocks

79

again, and he quivered with rage. 'Squit,' he shouted, and taking a vicious kick at the grass verge, he stamped off home.

It might have been pure coincidence, but when I had cause to call on Tom a few weeks later, I did notice that there wasn't one clock in the house that was going.

When Young 'Enry started buying up all the stuffed birds and animals that he could lay his hands on, the village sat up and took notice. Most cottages had at least one case of stuffed birds about the place, and some had a cat, or a squirrel, and there was even the odd fox or two. They were regarded as just so much junk by most people, and Young 'Enry had acquired quite a number of them before it became generally known that they were bringing a very high price indeed in the London auction rooms. John pricked up his ears when he heard the news, and decided that somehow he had to get in on the act. There wasn't any hope of his buying up any stuffed creatures in the village or surrounding area, as there wasn't a single person left who didn't know the real worth of their possessions by now. John was thinking big. He was going in for manufacturing. He obtained a heap of books from the mobile library and spent all his spare time studying them. It was obvious from the titles that he was trying to teach himself taxidermy, but Ben thought that he was studying to be a taxi driver until the chemicals started to arrive. Bottles of liquids with names that Ben had never heard of and certainly couldn't pronounce, scalpels and needles, and little boxes full of glass eyes, they poured in day after day. The little shed behind the cottage was crammed with them. When Ben at last realized what it was that John was up to, he groaned.

'Why not start off with a porcupine?' he asked. 'The spikes might put you off for life.'

John didn't answer, but carried on in his dogged way. He obtained a relatively unmarked weasel, recently killed, from Len, and locking himself in the shed one night, set to work.

'It's his head that's stuffed,' said Ben in despair. 'I'd rather see him get drunk every night than mess about with all them chemicals. At least getting drunk is a natural thing for a man to do.'

When John first showed his masterpiece to the world, the world greeted it with an awed silence. The sinuous shape of the weasel had somehow got lost in the treatment, and the animal that now crouched precariously on its plywood base

was a rotund, hump-backed little creature, with a head that was far too big for its body, and eyes that were far too big for its head. Its thin legs had begun to collapse under the weight of its body, and were so curved that the beast looked as though it had been holding on to some round object that had suddenly been pulled away from under it.

John showed the specimen proudly to Young 'Enry. 'How much will you give me for this?' he asked.

Young 'Enry looked at the thing and gasped. 'What is it?' he marvelled, 'a thalidomide coypu?' John was unabashed.

On his next visit to town John hawked the weird weasel from one dealer to another. At the end of a very long day he had to admit to himself that the world did not want his masterpiece at any price. He brought it into the pub again, when a few visitors were in, and after a few nasty rebuffs started trying to sell it for a pound to the only man who had not been downright rude about it.

'I don't want it for a pound,' said the man. 'I don't want it at all.'

'For goodness sake give him the thing for nothing,' said Ben. 'You're not bringing it back into the house again. It's started to smell, and the dog screams every time he sees it.' He looked at John and the fabulous beast with equal amounts of disgust. 'I don't know why you didn't take up pinning butterflies or something. This was a mad idea from the start.'

John paused as though struck by lightening. A smile crossed his face. 'Here,' he thrust the deformed animal on to the cringing man, 'it's a gift. You can have it.'

'But I don't want it,' shouted the man, with loathing in his voice, but John was already going out through the door.

'Butterflies,' he was saying to himself as he left, the old greedy gleam back in his eye. 'Butterflies, and moths as well. And dragonflies. I wonder if ladybirds. . . .'

He was gone. The stranger pushed the weasel from his lap and wiped his hands down the front of his coat. At the bar, Ben leaned his head in his hands, closed his eyes, and groaned.

When a local girl set her sights on a local man, the battle

was often a long drawn out affair, but in the end the female usually won. When Dolly Foster set her sights on John, Ben was delighted, the village was amused, and John was petrified. He stopped going to any of the dances that were held in the village hall, as all the other girls refused to dance with him. The word had gone around that he was spoken for. John himself didn't have any say in the matter.

As the congregation was leaving the church, Dolly Foster, who had been marking time deliberately, came out through the doors at John's side. Any stranger would have thought that the two were together, so close were their heads, and so animated their conversation.

'Your father is being neglected, John,' said Dolly as they came down the steps. 'As a Christian I just can't stand by and see the way that you let him go around. Just look at him limping along there, he looks like a mawkem on roller skates, the poor old thing.'

'My father,' said John, as rudely as he dared to someone that he was scared of, 'is not a stupid old faggot like some women I know of. He doesn't waste his money on a lot of clothes that ain't no good to him. He needs only two suits at his time of life, one for work, and one for church.'

'Oh really?' said Dolly, secretly delighted at having wrung such a lengthy answer from John, 'and which is he wearing today?'

It was one night during the following week that John came home to find Dolly sitting in the parlour darning socks. Old Ben was fully aware of the girl's motives, and he'd told her bluntly that he was behind her one hundred per cent. Meanwhile, he was glad to take advantage of her domestic ability, and hoped that in time John would grow to appreciate her too. Ben's socks were darned, and his shirts were mended. He was generally smartened up. But when it came to doing the washing, Dolly washed everything in sight, and that included John's garments. She pretended to be irritated that she had made such a mistake, but said that she might as well now iron them all, it would be easier than separating them into two heaps. By the next week it seemed normal for her to wash

83

and iron John's clothes along with Ben's. Tongues wagged in the village when Dolly's bicycle was seen standing outside Ben's cottage all night. Dolly had conveniently forgotten it and walked home. John was furious, and spoilt her plan the next time that she left it by wheeling it up the road and leaving it outside Charlie's cottage. Dolly didn't seem to mind. She never seemed to mind anything that John did or said. She simply carried on, hard working homely and efficient.

The weeks rolled by, and John came to accept the situation. He even began to enjoy it. Dolly would bake enormous pies and puddings, and they would be just leaving the oven as John came in through the door from his day's work. His shirts were in his drawer, neatly ironed and folded, and socks, rolled in pairs, were neatly placed alongside shirts of matching colour. John had to admit to himself that it was amazing that they had managed so long in the house without a woman's hand. He revelled in the girl's attention even more than Ben, but he was still surly in his manner to Dolly, and convinced that he would never be stupid enough to marry anyone, let alone the plain and homely little maid. But as he allowed himself to enjoy the cooking and the mending, he was quite unaware that the comfortable feeling that he was experiencing was all part of the plan. The trap was slowly closing on him.

One evening, after a week of wonderful meals, John came home to find no food waiting, and no Dolly. Ben was working away in the garden shed, whistling happily, and after waiting around for half an hour, and wondering whether he could ask his father where Dolly was without seeming too eager, he made himself a dripping sandwich and ate it in front of the empty hearth.

During the day Dolly had stood on the bridge and watched the young artist at work. It wasn't the first time that the young man had seen Dolly, but her plain and dumpy little figure didn't interest him at all, and he paid her no attention. That is, until she mentioned the possibility of buying one of his pictures.

'Excuse me,' she called to him, 'is that one for sale?'

The picture, a view of the bridge from the east, most certainly was for sale. The young painter leapt eagerly up the bank to show Dolly his work. He mentioned a price that Dolly wouldn't have dreamed of paying for the Mona Lisa, and she smiled sweetly up at him.

'I'm almost certain that this one will be suitable,' she said. 'It's for a very special present you see, and I'll have to check with the family. I promise to see you about it later.'

Dolly did see the painter later. She watched him go into the pub, and then she waited again until John's burly figure appeared at the end of the lane. He came stomping along, muttering to himself because he'd been unable to find a pair of socks that matched, and his shirt he had had to rescue from the soiled linen, as the others weren't ironed, and after weeks of having his clothes laid out for him, he didn't fancy the idea of ironing one for himself. He felt dishevelled and uncomfortable, and his temper wasn't too good. He had become accustomed to the soft life, and as he marched down the road to the pub, he didn't realize that that too was part of the plot. The trap had closed another inch or two on him.

When he entered the bar John did a quick double take. Then he stood transfixed for a good half a minute. In the corner Dolly and the young artist were sitting. Their heads were very close together as they examined one of the man's paintings. Dolly laughed coyly at something that the man had said and John took a deep breath. So that's why there hadn't been any steak and kidney pie, no socks, no shirts. He smacked his money down on the bar, but the couple in the corner didn't look up. As he gulped at his pint, he watched the two through the mirror. He noticed for the very first time what small teeth Dolly had, and how they sparkled when she laughed. He noticed how the curls of her hair framed her face in a way that was positively attractive.

The artist, convinced that he had the sale of the picture almost tied up, was turning on all his charm. Dolly for her part was acting in a manner that was quite out of character. She was squealing and giggling and looking up into the man's eyes with undisguised admiration. John had to admit to himself that the painter was rather a handsome type, even if he was as lean as a whippet. It was when Dolly placed a hand on the artist's arm as she emphasized some point, that John could stand it no longer. He swung around and crossed the bar in rage. He grasped Dolly with one podgy hand and heaving her from her seat, brought her to her feet in front of him.

'What the devil do you think you're doing,' he demanded, 'acting just like one of them cheap city girls. No girl of my acquaintance is going to come into a public bar unless she's with me.'

'Why John dear,' said Dolly, wide eyed, 'I didn't know that you could be so jealous. You are quite right of course, I'll go, but I'll see you later.' She leaned forward and planted a noisy kiss on his cheek and then she was gone.

For the second time in a few minutes John stood transfixed. This time he had heard the sound of the trap closing on him, and he was wondering how he had allowed himself to get in such a position when the young artist spoke. He had noted the width of John's shoulders and thought that it might not be a bad idea to clarify the situation.

'Er, excuse me,' he said nervously, watching the hefty fists clenching and unclenching with emotion, 'your fiancée and I were discussing the purchase of this painting. I wonder if you'd care to have a look at it yourself and give your opinion.'

John looked at the man as though he was something that had crawled out of the wall. 'No I wouldn't,' he said hastily. 'We don't like a load of pictures hanging around the house.' And then, when the rest of the customers in the bar chuckled, he could have bitten off his own tongue.

The months were sliding by in a way that they never seemed to do in the city. Perhaps because of the fact that the country people were more governed by the seasons than we were when we lived in town, there seemed to be more to look forward to in each month. As September approached, the whole village was looking forward to one particular event, the annual steam rally.

SIX

SEPTEMBER

THE patience that the average motorist displayed towards any steam driven vehicle always amazed me. Drivers who daily competed with each other and the rest of the world would pull into a gateway and wave affably when confronted with a hissing belching monster of a traction engine lumbering down a narrow country lane. The annual steam traction engine rally that was held in our village was marked by this same spirit of friendliness, and when Maggie and I paid our visit to the field, the proceedings were in full swing. Charlie, with a streak of grease across his bald head, was peering shortsightedly at a machine that was purring like a sewing machine. Ben, oil-can in hand, was perched high on a thumping, trembling monster, and was squirting oil over every part that moved. Percy, smart in a pair of very well pressed overalls, was giving rides on a miniature steam train. Cecil Pipes, who believed in talking to machines, was having a long conversation with a steam roller, and Whistling Jack, in his usual blue denims, was puffing out his cheeks and pursing his lips in competition with the general uproar. Miss Money, in an Ascot hat, was taking entrance money and selling programmes and toffee apples. Young 'Enry had a hoop-la stall, and Hubby was in charge of a bran tub, but as no one was showing any interest in their stalls they were both stretched out on the grass enjoying the sunshine. Everyone had his place, visitors abounded, and the afternoon seemed set for success.

In the mid afternoon it started to rain, one of those short

heavy showers with large warm drops. As a man the crowd fled towards the village hall. It was locked, but one door at the side was open. It led to a smallish room that was used for lesser functions, such as the meetings of the poetry reading circle, or the birdwatchers' club. The first ones to reach shelter were quickly pushed to the back of the room by the others as they shoved their way in. By the time they were all inside there was hardly an inch to spare. People were crammed together in such enforced intimacy that to many of them a mere drenching outside would have been infinitely more preferable.

'This is terrible, I must get out,' gasped Miss Money, gripping her now badly crushed hat. 'Let me out please.'

Whistling Jack, who was nearest to the door, which someone had thoughtlessly closed, grabbed the handle and tugged and rattled it. 'It, er, won't,' he said, red in the face. 'It's, er, stuck, or bolted, or locked or something.'

'Locked,' bellowed John tactlessly. 'Do you mean to say we're all locked in here?'

Three little ginger-headed children began to cry simultaneously, and their father, a big ginger-headed man, looked menacingly at Ben, whom he had met before.

'Give it a shove,' said Ben, and tried to move towards the door. The big ginger man moved after him. The three ginger children had each dropped their ice cream in their fear, and the smooth parquet floor was fast becoming an ice rink beneath the milling feet. As Ben started to move, his feet shot from under him and he sat down heavily. A large fat lady from the Women's Institute felt the brim of his hat touch the back of her skirt, and she turned round angrily.

'Oh, I see,' she said, looking down at Ben with loathing, 'a dirty old man.' And she cuffed him heavily about the head with her handbag. People were now milling and pushing about like a herd of frightened cattle. A spotty-faced youth who accidentally turned on his transistor radio at full volume would have been lynched had there been enough room, and an older man who had been foolish enough to enter the room with a pipe clenched between his teeth was fortunate to be able to remove it without the aid of a surgeon.

'I want to go,' the smaller of the ginger children kept wailing, and their big ginger father was growing angrier by the second.

'Open the blarsted door,' he roared at Ben, convinced that he was behind the trouble. The windows were beginning to mist up with condensation, and the temperature was rising rapidly. Outside, the shower had passed, and the hot sun was out again. Ben started to loosen his front collar stud, but hastily fastened it again when he saw the expression on the fat lady's face as she watched him. People were sitting down and standing up quite regularly now as the ice-cream had become more or less evenly distributed over the floor. The smallest ginger child stopped yelling 'I want to go'. But he kept on crying. Their noses told the crowd that he didn't want to go any more – he'd been. The big ginger man was still trying to edge his way closer to Ben, and Ben was trying to keep John in between him and the big ginger man.

'I'd like to know who locked the blarsted door,' said Percy, running his finger round the inside of his starched collar.

'So would I,' said the ginger man, and his knobbly fingers twitched as he cast another murderous glance towards Ben.

Maggie and I had made a dash for home as soon as the shower started. By the time that we had had a leisurely cup of tea the rain was over, and we strolled back to the field. The place was deserted. The steam engines stood unattended, some gasping and sighing, others shooting steam from the safety valves. The only sign of life was a group of boys near the entrance. Each one of them was eating a toffee apple, and each had at least another two or three in reserve. As Maggie and I approached, the lads scattered before us like leaves in a gale, and in no time at all there wasn't a boy to be seen.

We had walked completely around the field before Maggie drew my attention to the village hall. One room looked strange. From the outside it looked as though someone was using it as a laundry. The windows were absolutely streaming with condensation, and the muffled thumps and yells that came from inside sounded as though there was a rugby match going on. The door was locked, but the key was lying on a seat nearby. I took the key and unlocked the door, and then leapt back. The flood of damp humanity that poured out looked a great deal more dishevelled than the group of lads who had stayed out in the rain.

When the toffee apples were missed, and the reason for the locking of the door became apparent, Miss Money was as charitable as ever.

'Poor, poor boys,' she said, sighing. 'They must have been terribly hungry to do such a thing.' She looked around for support. 'They need an awful lot of food, growing boys do.'

'They need an awful lot of something else, as well,' said Percy, looking woefully down at the scratched toes of his best Sunday boots. The spotty youth with the radio went by, the radio bleating mutedly. In the general melée he had been thrown up against an equally spotty young girl, and they were now strolling hand in hand, a look of wonder on their two spotty faces.

Miss Money watched them, and blushed sweetly. 'Isn't it wonderful to see young people getting so much enjoyment out of life?' she said.

'Yes,' said Ben, gripping his stick fiercely, 'but if I see any young people about today with toffee apples, I'm a-goin' to have a bit of enjoyment myself.'

To one side of the Post Office, growing up the outside wall of an outhouse, there was a grapevine. It was a huge thing, with a main stem that was thicker than a man's arm, and was obviously very old indeed. Maggie and I watched with surprise as grapes formed, and grew large. As we never tended the vine in any way, this fruit that nature provided was regarded as a bonus. They were not sweet enough to be eaten as a dessert grape, but were so large and juicy that they were ideal for Maggie's hobby of wine making. She made full use of them, and produced a wine that had a distinctive flavour and that became very popular indeed with the local housewives. It soon became known in the village as 'that quare old wine' and whenever anyone used that phrase, it meant Maggie's wine, and no other. I didn't like it myself, preferring a glass of beer any time, but Maggie and her friends got through gallon after gallon of the stuff, Maggie using her recipe that allowed the wine to be drunk only a few weeks after bottling. It was pretty strong stuff, even then, and it made us wonder what it would be like after keeping for a twelve-month.

One evening, when the kitchen and lounge were full of women each holding a glass of the 'quare wine', Maggie asked with a laugh who had named the wine, and why 'quare'.

'Why, don't you know my dear?' asked one farmer's wife. 'It's because of the way the vine was planted, all them years ago. It's growing on the grave of a goat, you see. It always pays to bury an animal under a vine. A dog ain't bad, and a sheep's pretty good, but a goat's best of all. It gives it strength and flavour, that's why your wine has a flavour all of its own.' The other ladies chorused their agreement. Maggie turned slightly green, and put down her glass.

She made plenty of the 'quare old wine' after that, and many people enjoyed drinking it, but she never drank another glass of it herself since then.

When Mrs Peckham developed a limp, Maggie and I mentioned it to each other but didn't say anything to the lady herself, waiting for her to tell us about her condition, as most elderly people love to do. However, after she had missed calling in for her widow's pension for the fourth consecutive week, I called in to see her when I was passing. I found her sitting in an armchair with her feet up on a stool.

'Come in,' she called cheerfully, as she saw me through the window. I ducked my way into the low room and took a seat near her.

Mrs Peckham, after a few polite opening remarks, mentioned her limp, and the fact that it had got worse. She explained in a matter of fact way, with no trace of bitterness or self-pity, that she had an incurable condition, and would get steadily worse. She said that she would soon have to use a wheelchair, and would eventually become bedfast. 'But that's another day,' she said. 'We've enough to worry about from day to day without crossing our bridges before we come to them.'

She spoke more cheerfully about herself than did most people who were in good health, and I found her a fascinating person to listen to. Since she was no longer able to work in her garden, which had been her pride and joy, she had taken up needlework, and she showed me her first attempts at embroidery. The stitches were so large and clumsy, and the effort that had gone into the work so obvious, that I was struck dumb, and felt a flood of pity for this elderly lady, who had no one in the whole world that she could call a relative, and who was being so brave about her illness.

'Don't be afraid to laugh,' she said, laughing herself. 'I never was very good with a needle I'm afraid, even as a schoolgirl, and I hardly think that I've improved over the years since then.' She stroked the material slowly. 'Still,' she said, 'I've got plenty of time to practise.'

I called on Mrs Peckham weekly from then on, taking her pension and any odds and ends that she needed from the store. We would talk for a while on each visit, and slowly I learnt quite a lot about her. The more I got to know her the more I admired her, and the sight of her stiffened fingers working away at some clumsy piece of needlework always moved me.

In answer to her questions, I told her how Maggie and I had come to live in the district, and she nodded when I told her of the way we felt about the city life we used to lead, that life was somehow meant to be different, and that we had been living at a pace that had been altogether too hectic, and how we enjoyed so much the slower, more peaceful life that we now led. She had tried city life for herself, she said, when she had been young, and the only good thing that had come out of it had been the meeting of her late husband. They had married and then returned to the country and started a small chicken farm, and the only regrets that they had ever had was that they had wasted so many years of their lives chasing money in the city, when the life that they really enjoyed had been here in the country, waiting for them.

Maggie and I knew that Mrs Peckham was due to go into hospital, but the way that it came about we didn't have time to see her and say good-bye. She didn't go into a local hospital either, but one that was three and a half hours' driving away, making visiting impossible except on Bank Holiday weekends.

The news of her going was brought to us by her nearest neighbour, who also brought a small package addressed to me. On opening it I found one of those small squares of embroidered material such as could be seen hanging on the walls of many of the cottages. Maggie said that it was called a sampler. The embroidery took the form of a verse, which said:

> Man should not live in constant haste,
> and tremble at the bell,
> 'til life becomes a kind of prolonged illness.
> He should turn away, and find somewhere
> a better place to dwell,
> With slow clock-ticking, dust-collecting stillness.

The needlework was faultless.

Weasel Peters was aptly named. He was a small brown man with small dark eyes and a pointed face. He wore brown clothes and brown boots and was as well camouflaged as any weasel in the wild. But the most unusual thing about him was his ears, which were the smallest ears that I have ever seen, and were so close to his small smooth head that he did indeed look very much like a weasel. He was the chief poacher in a nearby village, and didn't turn up in our village very often, being in competition with Len, but now and again he would make an excursion to our pub, in order to keep abreast of current affairs.

It was on one such visit that Weasel lost his gold piece. This was a gold sovereign that he had carried on the end of his watch chain ever since he had left school, as his father had done before him. When he discovered his loss Weasel scoured the district, retracing his steps and searching in all the likely places, but he was unsuccessful. He bemoaned his luck over the bar of the village pub, showing the naked end of the chain to the customers and offering a reward to anyone who might find the coin. It could be easily identified, he said, by its age, and by the little loop of metal by which it had been attached to its chain. It was pointed out to Weasel that the discovery of the coin might cause him some embarrassment, as it might be used to prove his presence on property where his presence was not strictly legal. Weasel shrugged, and said that he wanted the coin back wherever it was found, and that he couldn't be hanged for trespassing. It was then suggested that if the coin was found by Len on his territory, the retribution that followed might be a good deal worse than anything that the law might hand out. Weasel was silent after that, and someone changed the subject.

It was shortly after this conversation that Len himself came into the bar. He nodded to his competitor and orderd a drink. As he paid he spilt several coins out on to the bar.

'Here,' said George, 'isn't that one a sovereign?'

'Yes,' said Len, 'worth quite a bit nowadays I suppose.'

'It's got a bit of a link on it, where it should go on a chain,' said George.

'Yes,' said Len, 'one of these days I'll buy a decent bit of chain and fix it on.'

The bar held its breath, but silence followed. Weasel was thinking furiously. It was obvious to him that Len had found the sovereign somewhere on his patch, and was going to taunt him with it. Well hang him. He wasn't going to ask him for it. He wasn't going to own it even.

During the next few days the bitterness ate into Weasel's heart. The more he thought about Len the more he hated him. He set his snares on Len's patch, in spite of the gentleman's agreement that they had to keep off each other's stamping ground. 'All's fair in love and war,' he said to himself as he took a fine hare from the wire noose that had trapped it. It was then that he noticed the footprints. They were all around the one bush, and Weasel guessed correctly that the footprints were Len's. He knew that Len would have a hiding place somewhere on his patch where he could leave a gun hidden from one day to the next, the same as he did himself. Perhaps this was it. He searched around, dropping on all fours and sticking his head under the leaves of the bush like a terrier, and at last he found it. The gun was very well hidden and covered with loose earth and leaves, and was carefully wrapped in a sheet of green oilskin material. The joy that Weasel got from his find was tremendous. He laughed aloud, and then sat back and looked at the weapon, trying to make up his mind what to do with it. As he sat there, the sound of running water came to his ears. He slapped his knee. That was it, the river. He carried the gun to the bank, and when he got there he made another discovery. Lying half hidden in the reeds at the water's edge was a punt. Len's punt, it must be. Weasel was delighted by his luck. It was surely fate that had led him to these two discoveries, and it was up to him to make the most of them. He raised the gun, and with vicious blows he smashed the bottom of the punt through. Then, as the old boat settled slowly into the mud, he flung the gun into deeper water in the middle of the river.

When Weasel got to the pub Len was already in there, laughing and joking with Percy and George. 'Ah, Weasel,' said Len, turning, 'I hear that you've lost your old sovereign. I've got one here that I've no use for. You can have it for the price of a couple of pints if you like. It's not as old as the one that you lost, of course, but it is a gold sovereign.'

Weasel gaped at Len in silence. Was this some kind of a trick? He was stuck for words, but George was not.

'No need for you to do that, Len,' he said. 'A sovereign is worth a sight more than a couple of pints, as you well know. In any case, I found Weasel's coin under the seats here in the bar. Here you are Weasel, look after it in future.' He slapped the coin down on the bar in front of the speechless poacher. Weasel picked up the coin and went slowly out of the bar, still not speaking. As far as I know, although he still poached in the area now and again, Weasel never visited the village pub again.

Simon Stead was a very quiet type, and we didn't see very much of him in the Post Office. He was a retired schoolmaster, and could be seen early in the mornings walking his dog around the village long before most of the villagers were out of their beds. Simon was deaf and wore an earpiece in his left ear that had a wire running from it to his top pocket. One day, on one of his rare visits to the shop, I noticed that the wire was hanging loosely from his ear, having become detached from the apparatus in his pocket. I raised my voice and pointed this out to him and said that I hoped that he hadn't damaged his hearing aid.

'Oh no,' he said, 'no fear of that. You see I'm only slightly deaf, and I found out long ago that when people see this wire they automatically raise their voices. I haven't bought any batteries for this thing for years.'

His wife was the opposite in temperament to Simon. She was a quick, energetic old girl and she bobbed in and out of the shop several times each day, like a jack-in-the-box. Every week she bought several ounces of a very strong tobacco, and she would complain bitterly about the expense, often saying that she would have to get Simon to try to give up smoking altogether, and certainly would do so if the stuff went up again. It was months before Maggie and I learnt that Simon Stead didn't smoke, and never had done. It was Mrs Stead herself who incurred all the expense, sitting by the fire, knitting and puffing on an old clay pipe.

It was Simon, out for his early morning exercise, who discovered the hole that had appeared overnight in the middle of the playing field. It was fortunate that it had appeared when it did, as there was no danger of anyone falling down it at that hour. Simon peered down the hole, and was surprised to see that it was brick lined, like a well. He couldn't see the bottom, but could tell that it was very deep, so he collected his dog and went off to inform the village policeman. By mid-morning the council had sent round Teddy

Collins and his gang, and they swarmed over the site with enthusiasm. They erected a circle of tubular metal barriers around the hole and placed a great number of warning signs about the place. Then, not having had any further instructions, they went away, leaving a ring of red lamps ready to be lit at night.

The stories that circulated around the village all differed slightly in detail, but agreed on the main facts. The well was one that had collapsed three generations ago, killing its owner. At that time there had been no playing field, the well being behind the man's house. He had been drawing water from the well when the whole top had caved in. The man and the heavy old pump had crashed down the well together.

' 'Twas the weight,' said the old men, knowingly, 'those old pumps were solid lead, you know, 'cos lead was dirt cheap in them days.'

'Yes, you're right,' it was agreed. 'They weighed tons.'

John pricked up his ears when he heard this. He knew that all the existing pumps in the village were made of lead, and that lead brought a very good price, but they were just ordinary little pumps, and if the one that had fallen down the well was a great deal bigger, then it would be worth quite a lot of money. He pictured in his mind all the precious metal lying uselessly at the bottom of a hole in the ground, and he grew restless.

Discreet inquiries brought forth two opposing opinions. One was that the body of the unfortunate man would have been hauled out of the well and given a Christian burial, and the other that the body would have been left there and the well sealed, as it would have been too dangerous to recover it, and people weren't as fussy about that kind of thing in those days as we are today. A search was made through the village graveyard, but it failed to reveal any tombstone with information concerning the victim or the accident. The vicar was called on, but he could be of no help, as the man's name was not known, nor was the exact date of the accident. Although half the village swore that the body was left down the well, and the other half were equally certain that it was not, no one suggested for a minute that the old pump had been removed, and as he listened to the villagers, John grew even more restless. It was known for a fact that a large bore had been sunk in the village around the turn of the century, and it was generally assumed that this was the cause of the well now being dry. It kept springing to John's mind that the dryness of the well would make the recovery of the pump such a simple business. It could be sawn up into easily manageable pieces at the bottom of the well, lead is soft stuff to saw, and perhaps one or two strong men could manage to haul the bits to the surface without too much difficulty. All day as he worked the ideas kept running through his mind, and in the end his restlessness became unbearable.

It was two o'clock in the morning when the two shadowy figures flitted across the playing field towards the well. 'Did you remember to bring the hacksaw?' asked Whistling Jack in a whisper.

'Course I did,' answered John, determined to keep his place as leader of the expedition. 'Course I did. What do you take me for?'

Whistling Jack didn't answer, but thought to himself that if it hadn't been for the width of John's shoulders, he would have told him several times before now just what he did take him for. Whistling Jack was carrying a large coil of rope, and the fact that he was out of breath already, while John carried nothing heavier than a hacksaw seemed to him to be a little unfair. He held his tongue though. If a man is going to be relied on to pull you up out of the bowels of the earth, one doesn't want to offend him too much until after he has performed the said feat.

They approached the edge of the hole with caution. By the dim light of the red lamps they dragged one of the tubular metal barriers and placed it across the mouth of the well. The barriers were robust constructions that Teddy Collins and his men had made up out of scaffolding poles, and were easily capable of supporting the weight of a man and several hundredweight besides. The rope was looped over the metal pole and dropped down into the well. Whistling Jack placed his foot in the loop at the end of the rope and took a firm grip.

'Lower away,' he whispered, 'and take it steady. I'll switch on my lamp when I've dropped down a bit, so as people won't see the light.' John lowered his partner slowly down into the depths, and leaning back away from the hole, soon lost sight and sound of him.

When Whistling Jack switched on his lamp he found himself dropping steadily down into a green, moss-covered pipe that seemed to grow narrower the lower he went. He didn't like the sensation at all. He couldn't make out how much farther he had to go, and the spinning and turning at the end of the rope made him feel quite ill. Heights he didn't mind, and he had thought that depths would be very much the same, but he realized now that they were very much different. He called up the shaft softly to John to stop for a minute so that he could shine his lamp around and get his bearings. John didn't hear him, and Jack went bobbing on his way, turning this way and that as he did so.

When a slight projection on the wall appeared beneath his foot, Jack automatically allowed his weight to rest on it and stop his descent. Then he called up again to John. 'Hang on will you. Hold it for a minute.' John heard the voice this time, and he felt the rope go slack. Thinking that Whistling Jack had reached the bottom he eased the rope from his shoulders and stepped to the edge of the hole.

When Jack's foot slipped off the moss-covered stone he had only about six feet to fall, although he didn't know it at the time. The fall was enough to wind him, and to scare the wits out of him. He sat up on the mossy stones and damp silt at the bottom of the well and bellowed up at John. 'What the devil's going on? Why did you let me fall?' He fumbled with his lamp and was relieved to find that it still worked. John, peering down into the depths of the well, saw like a glimpse into the underworld, a grotto bathed in green light and a greenish coloured upturned face mouthing up at him.

Ignoring Whistling Jack's questions he shouted down a couple of his own. 'Is there anything down there? Any pump, any lead?'

'Nothing,' yelled Jack, 'now pull me up and get me out of this.' There was absolute silence for a second or two, and fear ran up Jack's spine as he realized the position that he was in. No one in the world knew that he was down the hole except John, and John was the very last person in the world that Jack would have chosen to rely on. 'Do you hear me?' he bawled up the shaft, not caring now whether the whole village heard him or not. 'Pull me up. Now!'

'I can't,' said John, 'the rope's fallen down there with you.'

Jack screamed, and then steadied himself with a tremendous effort. He could see now, as he flashed his lamp around, that the rope was indeed coiled around him at the bottom of the well, and he could also see that there was no possible way for him to get up to the top again without a rope. 'In my van,' he shouted, mouthing each word slowly, separately and carefully, 'there are ropes. Get them.'

'Right,' answered John. 'Won't be long.'

Whistling Jack didn't answer, his eyes were closed and he was praying.

Pipes and Shorty approached the well from the opposite direction, and didn't see John's figure hurrying away into the gloom. When Jack heard them arrive he knew that it couldn't be John back so soon and he could also hear two whispering voices. He put out his lamp and crouched at the bottom of the hole, shivering with cold and fear. There was an awful lot of scuffling and muttering going on at the top, and quite a lot of loose soil fell down the hole and on to Whistling Jack. Eventually a figure blocked his view of the night sky, and he knew that someone was coming down towards him on the end of a rope. As the figure came nearer he realized that he couldn't very well remain concealed until the man reached the bottom, so he switched on his lamp and called softly up the shaft, 'hey there.' The figure was having the same trouble that he had had, turning and spinning on the end of the rope. As soon as he had spoken Jack saw a change in the outline of the figure above him. It stiffened, became rigid, and one of its hands let go of the rope and reached out to the wall of the shaft to steady itself. It then uttered a sound that was quite unlike anything that Jack had ever heard, excepting perhaps the sound that the architect's assistant had made the year before when he had fallen from the belfry of the village church. It was rather like the sound of air being drawn into a gigantic pair of bellows, but was much, much louder.

When Shorty heard the voice calling to him from the depths of the well, he steadied himself as best he could, and looked down past his own feet. His eyes bulged, and a small voice inside his skull screamed. He saw a green-faced figure glowing at the bottom of the hole, its hideous face gibbering up at him. It couldn't possibly be human, and his mind flew to the conversations about the body, and whether or not it had been removed from the well. 'Stop,' he screamed at the top of his voice to Pipes. 'Get me up. Pull me out.' He stole another glance downwards and saw that the figure was now reaching up its hand towards him, its face still mouthing horribly. Shorty didn't wait for Pipes to pull him up. With a strength that he didn't know he possessed he went back up the rope hand over hand with the speed of a scalded cat. At the surface he leapt out, and brushing Pipes aside with an incoherent sob, went tearing off over the fields in a homeward direction. Pipes, baffled by this behaviour, took a look down the well for himself. He was just in time to catch half a glimpse of what might have been a green apparition, as Whistling Jack put out his lamp again to save the batteries. Pipes started back, and then peered down again. Had he seen what he had thought he had seen? The thing was gone now, if it had ever been there in the first place, and if it hadn't been there, what had caused Shorty to take off like that? He coiled up his rope thoughtfully, and before he left the well, took another long look into its depths. There was nothing to be seen. He had known that there would be nothing. He kicked a large turf down the hole in disgust, and turned away. He didn't hear the muffled howl that followed.

When Whistling Jack told Maggie and me and the Post Office customers about the episode of the well, it was long enough afterwards for him to be able to laugh about it. He was certain that there had been nothing of value at the bottom of the shaft, and the council men had filled in the hole since then, and rammed the filling well down, so no one could contradict him. Grass was now growing over the site again, and even John seemed to have forgotten about it. But Whistling Jack still felt that he had had the worst part of the action in the affair, and was determined to get back at John in some small way. He and John had plans to club together and buy an electronic metal detector between them, and hunt for buried treasure in a big way. Jack said that he had known about this before the men had filled in the hole. 'I threw enough old iron down there to build a battleship,' he said. 'There were a couple of old bedsteads, a motor bike frame, and a dozen of them old metal fence posts. They're only about two foot down, and I reckon that the detector will pick 'em up all right. I want to just wander across the field, sort of casual like, with this detector thing going. I can't wait to see John's face when he thinks that there really is a great heap of metal still lying down at the bottom of that well.'

We had in the village dogs of every size, shape and colour. From Granny Coster's little Jack Russell terrier, sitting on his rooftop and challenging anything on four legs, to Len's huge old labrador, that could carry eggs in its soft mouth and lay them unbroken at your feet. They were all good dogs, and neither we nor the villagers had any trouble at all with them, which was surprising when you consider all the many different forms of livestock that were kept. To every rule there is an exception, and where dogs were concerned Young 'Enry's dog was the exception. It was a medium sized, blotchy coated, highly strung animal, with the unfortunate habit of picking up and carrying off home any article that was not firmly nailed down. At first Young 'Enry had been embarrassed by the dog's habits and had tried his best to return to its rightful owner any article that his dog acquired. He had in fact often called in at the Post Office to enquire whether anyone had complained about the disappearance of a baby's rattle, or a photograph of Lord Kitchener, or a surgical truss.

After a time, when the dog began bringing home the washing from people's clothes lines, Young 'Enry gave up. After one terrible day when he had toured the village with a couple of pairs of outsize flannel bloomers, impeccably patched, to which no female would lay claim, he took to disposing of the loot secretly, and denying all knowledge of the dog's plundering.

When the contractors moved in and started digging the trench for the main sewer down the middle of the village street, things became rather serious as far as the dog's activities were concerned. The animal soon discovered that the men were easy pickings, and he could often be seen loping homeward carrying a lunchbox, or tools, or even a rolled up working jacket in his mouth. At my suggestion, Young 'Enry bought a cat's bell and attached it to the dog's collar. It wouldn't stop the dog stealing, but it would give the intended victim some warning of the dog's approach, or so we thought. The bell worked very well for everyone except those very people that it had been intended to help. The villagers soon grew to know the sound of the bell, and chased the dog off before it could get its teeth into any of their possessions, but the noise of the machinery that the sewer men used was so loud that it drowned the tinkling of the bell, and deprived of all other sources of booty, the dog plagued the workmen daily, and soon became public enemy number one as far as the gang were concerned.

When the dog disappeared, Young 'Enry was the only person in the whole village to show any concern. Even the tender-hearted and forgiving Miss Money had lost all sympathy for the animal after it had dragged her underwear, which had been drying in the privacy of her kitchen, through the village street in broad daylight. When Young 'Enry asked Ben and Percy whether they had seen his dog they replied that if he kept the thing tied up he would know where it was. 'Enry said that he thought it unnatural to keep a dog tied up, but it was answered that his dog wasn't natural anyway. After the sewer had been installed, and the trench filled in, the men came back with a lorry and shovelled all the excess

soil and rubble into it. They made a very good attempt at
cleaning up the road, and swept up every last scrap of
rubbish and loaded it. Ben and I were idly watching, and as
we did so, I thought that I heard a familiar sound. When I
mentioned this, the workmen said that they had heard nothing, and went on shovelling. Ben, too, assured me gravely that
I had been mistaken, and I let it go, but looking back, I am

sure now that as the last few scraps of dirt were being thrown into the lorry, I heard something roll, and tinkle, just like one of those little cat bells that I had sold to Young 'Enry.

I had assumed that once the summer was over, things would be rather quiet in the village, especially for the farm workers. As usual, I was wrong. Community activities used up any spare time that the male workers had, their women-folk saw to that, and there were constant repairs to be made to farm machinery, farm roads, and farm buildings. It was in the month of October that I tried my hand at the sort of unskilled manual labour that so many of the men of the village did for their living, and I found it a good deal harder than I had ever imagined.

SEVEN

OCTOBER

It was the village schoolmistress who first raised the question of the footpath across Lady Blanche's woodland. In seeking new routes for nature rambles for her pupils, she had unearthed some very old papers in the school that showed that in times gone by there had been in existence a footpath that had been in regular use by the children of the village. The teacher felt that if Lady Blanche was approached in the right way, she might allow the path to be opened up once again. It was decided that the best way to tackle the rather tricky task was for the Village Hall committee to send a letter to Lady Blanche pointing out that they knew full well that they had no legal right to claim a public right of way, but asking her if the path could be reopened in the interests of the village as a whole. When the committee met again, Joe, the Lady's gardener, attended. He read out a short letter from his employer, which to everyone's surprise said that she would be delighted to see the footpath opened up again, and that she would leave all the arrangements to her gardener, Joe. She made only one condition, and that was that the villagers themselves should show their interest in the project by voluntarily undertaking some of the manual work that would be involved in clearing the overgrown path. She would contribute the labour of Joe, who would supervise the volunteers. Joe went on to say that the woodland in question was continually being trespassed upon, by poachers and courting couples, and it had been decided that things would be a good deal easier for Lady Blanche's gamekeeper if there was a clearly defined area that could be used by the public, and a good fence around the rest. Old Charlie nodded his head in agreement, and said that young courting couples should have a place where their elders could keep an eye on them. This remark brought him a nudge from Dolly Foster that knocked his glasses off.

On the Wednesday afternoon I used the half-day closing to do my share of the voluntary work. I wrapped myself up in an assortment of the oldest clothes that I could find, and looking more like a tramp than anything else, I set off. I worked away among the trees alone. Most of the other volunteers were at their places of work and the pensioners were no doubt sleeping off their midday beer. The branches and bushes had all been hacked back and a way cleared right through the wood. The task now was to make the going underfoot a little smoother. A few inches below the surface of leaves and compost there was the remnants of an old path. This was mostly a layer of hard-packed flints. The spade would slice through the leaves and soil easily enough, and would then strike the flints, jarring the hands painfully and sending up sparks. My hands, softened by shop work, soon blistered, and I cast off some of the ragged clothes as the work become warmer than I had anticipated. I worked as fast as I possibly could, but after a couple of hours had to admit to myself that if I left things as they were, the other workers wouldn't even know that I had been there. I attacked the ground again, wondering how it was that Ben and his friends could make such work appear easy, and before very long my blistered hands began to bleed.

It was about then that the old man came slowly along the path towards me. We passed the time of day, and he remarked that it looked like hard work, and that a downpour of rain might soften up the ground for me. I replied that no amount of rain would soften up the flints, and he took a closer look at the subsoil.

'You're right,' he said. 'Your best plan is to dodge this job altogether. I've worked all my life at the big hall in the next village, and I know what I'm talking about. You go to your doctor and get a note saying you've got lumbago. They can't prove that you haven't, you know. Give the note to Lady Blanche and take a couple of days off. By the time that you get back to work, one of them loony week-end volunteers will have cleared this lot up for you.'

The knife grinder, who made periodical calls around the villages, did a reasonably good trade with the housewives, sharpening their knives and scissors, but found that most of the menfolk were reluctant to pay him for doing a job that they considered they could do equally well for themselves, if only they had the equipment. The grinder's equipment consisted of a large tricycle that he laboriously pedalled from site to site. When he set up his workshop he merely stood the rear wheels of the tricycle on a stand, which lifted them clear of the road, and fitted a pulley belt that drove the grinding wheels themselves. He would then pedal away for hours on end, sharpening anything that came his way, and for a very small charge indeed.

Ben had a couple of axes that needed sharpening but he was determined not to pay, so when the grinder set up stall near Ben's cottage, the old man struck a bargain with him. He offered the grinder a meal of pork cheese in exchange for the use of the grinding equipment during the man's lunch break. Pork cheese is a jelly-like mass made out of all the left-over bits and pieces from a pig, all boiled together and moulded in tubs and pots while still warm and liquid. It should, I suppose, really be called brawn. Maggie and I had tasted it after it had been praised to us by the locals, but found that we didn't like it at all, and the fact that there were small hairs from the hide of the pig in every mouthful made Maggie shudder at the mere mention of it. The knife grinder, however, like the villagers, regarded it as a delicacy and after considering that the amount of time that Ben would get on his equipment would be in direct ratio to the amount of food that he would receive, accepted the offer. He sat on the verge, munching away, while Ben pedalled furiously, determined to get through as much work as was possible during the time allotted to him. He had got the grinding wheel revolving at a good speed when John came out of the cottage to watch him.

'You're holding it all wrong,' said John, meaning the axe, which was showering sparks high into the air. 'I won't be able to use it at all if you go and ruin the edge like that.'

'Squit,' said Ben, and pedalled faster.

'Here,' said John, 'let me show you.' He tried to grab the axe from his father.

'Gerroff,' yelled Ben, and leaned away from him. The rocking motion thus caused was enough to jerk the tricycle from its stand and, as the wheels came into contact with the road, the ungainly machine set off, first with a jerk, and then settling down to a steady pace, with a now wide-eyed Ben crouched aboard. The road sloped gently down from Ben's cottage and within seconds the weird machine was going rather too fast for him to consider jumping off, his game leg not being as flexible as he would have liked it to have been.

'Put the blarsted brake on!' shouted the knife grinder after him as he swerved along the road. Ben grabbed at a lever in response, but all that this did was to transfer the drive from one grinding wheel to another. There was no free wheel on the vehicle, and sparks flew as the axe that Ben was still gripping came into accidental contact with the abrasive surface.

As Ben and the now speeding contraption neared Len's cottage, the big old labrador was idly strolling out through the gate, pausing to sniff at the gatepost.

'Gerrout,' bawled Ben. 'Gerrout o' the way, blast you.' The dog looked round and saw a wild-eyed figure bearing down on him, a figure that was astride a machine the likes of which the dog had never seen before, a machine that rattled like a machine gun and sent sparks flying through the air. The dog flattened its ears and the whites of its eyes showed. Not having time to retreat back into the safety of its own garden, the dog had no option but to run away from

the menacing machine. This he did, but reluctantly, looking back over his shoulder and growling as he ran. The dog
crossed the road, sensibly enough, and left Ben and the
machine ample room to pass, but Ben, without meaning to,
swerved across the road in pursuit. The dog was now
frightened and he shot off down the road at a terrific speed,
Ben reluctantly followed, his speed also increasing.

As Percy, driving his ancient car, turned the corner, he
was faced by Len's dog running straight down the middle
of the not too wide road, straight towards him. Percy braked
and swerved, perhaps not as quickly as he might have done,
and he managed to miss the dog, which shot into the nearest
gateway, seeking any refuge from this insane human and
his fearful machine. Percy and Ben were now facing each
other, and closing at speed. By great good fortune they each
swerved in the opposite direction and Percy brought the old
car to rest with its bonnet nestling deep in a privet hedge.
Ben had gradually run up the sloping verge, losing quite a
bit of his speed as he did so, and had finally fallen from the
machine when it tipped over in the same gateway as the unfortunate dog had hidden in.

'You stupid old fool,' shouted Percy at Ben. 'Why can't
you ride an ordinary bike like everyone else?' The knife
grinder came panting up, accompanied by John.

'Oh law, oh gaw,' wheezed Ben, rubbing his bruised
shins with his hands. He was crouched down in this position when the old labrador made his bid for freedom. Seeing that Ben wasn't nearly as frightening now that he was
separated from the awful machine, the dog lost some of
his fear and regained some of his anger. It rushed at Ben
from the rear, bit him savagely, and then bolted homeward. 'Aaah, oh law,' yelled Ben, grabbing at the seat of
his trousers.'

'Good dog,' said Percy, John and the knife grinder
together.

When Granny Coster's cat began making a nuisance of
itself half the village complained. The cat certainly had a

much louder voice than its size implied, and its amorous yowlings carried through the night air to an amazing distance. It made its noises at the other end of the village to Granny Coster's cottage, and Granny simply couldn't bring herself to believe that her little pet could be the cause of so much trouble. She was convinced that it was a case of mistaken identity and that in time things would sort themselves out. Why the tom had decided to leave his own soul mate and begin wandering abroad we couldn't tell, but many a haggard worker threatened to shoot the cat if Granny didn't keep it locked up at night and allow him to get his sleep, and I think that if Granny had not been such a dear old lady the threat would have been carried out, and without warning. As it was, the only missiles that struck the cat were boots and books and the odd ashtray. Whistling Jack tried lying in wait for the cat with his catapult, but after he had broken his third window the neighbours begged him to stop, and one of them, who happened to be deaf, threatened to shoot Jack if he didn't stop disturbing his sleep.

Pipes, who had his early morning postman's round, had to rise earlier than most of us, and after suffering in silence for some weeks, decided to take action. The locals meanwhile had tried everything, from a special mixture of secret ingredients that was supposed to deter cats by its smell, to a couple of angry dogs, roused from their slumbers by an equally angry master. The former had had no effect at all, apart from causing the windows of the village school to be left open all day, whatever the weather, and the latter proved to be a deal noisier than the cat, the dogs barking loudly at their owner for having disturbed them.

When Pipes promised that he would stop all the trouble, and that he wouldn't have to shoot the cat, we were all doubtful, but within a couple of nights the yowlings ceased, and within a couple of weeks the village had forgotten all about the cat.

I tried on several occasions to find out from Pipes how he had achieved this remarkable success, but he wouldn't talk. It wasn't until the night that he won the big Bingo prize that I learnt the truth. He had been celebrating his luck, and had had more to drink than was usual for him. I called in at the pub just before closing time and managed to persuade him to have just one more for the road. As he was walking home and not driving, he accepted, and as he drank I asked him again. 'How on earth did you manage to get rid of that old tom cat without shooting it? We haven't heard it since, although I've seen it around in the daytime. However you achieved it, it was certainly a very successful operation.'

Pipes winked in an inebriated fashion, and tapped the side of his nose with a forefinger. 'A little know-how and a lot of patience, that's all it took,' he said. When I looked mystified, he came closer, and looking around to make sure that no one else was listening, confided in a whisper. 'I got everything prepared,' he said, 'and then I waited up for him. I grabbed him as he was getting up on to the roof of the shed. I stuffed him head first into the Wellington boot that I had ready. Two quick nicks with my old razor was all that it took, and bor, didn't he belt off home sharpish when I let him go. A successful operation you called it, well it was, and the scalpel was my old razor and the operating table was my old Wellington boot.' He laughed. 'You know,' he said, 'I'll bet that right now that old cat can't remember just what it was he was a-lookin' for when he used to come to this end of the village.'

Some weeks after the contractors had finished laying the main sewer the roadmen came along to resurface the village street. These men were not contractors, but council men under the directions of their foreman, Teddy Collins. The ditches and trenches that the sewer men had filled in had all settled and sunk to such an extent that the whole village was pleased to see the roadmen. Our cars had been taking a lot of punishment, and even cyclists were complaining. Several of the villagers had taken it upon themselves to fill in the holes nearest their own homes, and had used a variety of unsuitable materials, making matters worse by creating little hills to go with the holes.

When they started their work, Teddy Collins and his gang were treated to cups of tea, home made scones, and the odd glass of home made beer, but as they neared the end of their labours, the friendly attitude of the villagers disappeared.

At the roads leading into and out of the village signs had been placed. These read simply, SLOW LOOSE CHIPPINGS. We did drive slowly. All the villagers except two young hotheads on motorbikes drove very slowly. And when a faster car passed us, we got our windscreens broken. One by one the windscreens of nearly every cautious and reasonable driver in the village was broken, and the only cars that escaped this fate were the cars of the strangers who ignored the signs and speeded through the village. The injustice was apparent to all. Letters were penned to local papers and reporters even visited the village and noted down the comments of some of the more outspoken members of the community. Letters flooded in to the local council. Grumbling letters, accusing letters, and a few threatening letters. As is usual in such cases, nothing whatsoever was done. A spokesman for the council stated in a press interview that the broken windscreens were caused by speeding, and were the responsibility of the drivers involved. We all knew that, of course, probably a lot better than he did, but what he omitted to say was that the screens that were broken were of the slow driving majority not the odd speeding driver. Also, as was pointed out time after time, if the council hadn't left all the loose chippings about in the first place, there wouldn't have been any broken windscreens at all. Other letters appearing in the papers made it obvious that we were not alone in our complaints. From other villages, from all over the county, and from all over the country, they showed that people were experiencing the same trouble. Every year thousands of pounds worth of windscreens were being shattered, the bulk of them belonging to ordinary people who had committed no offence at all. All over the country too, the councils' replies were the same. A spokesman bleated the obvious fact that the breakages were caused by people driving too fast over the litter of chippings that the council had caused to be left there in the first place.

In our little village things got to a ridiculous state. A couple of cars had their windscreens smashed when they were parked outside the Post Office, and their drivers inside, shopping. A cottage had its window broken too, its only crime being that it was situated near a bend in the road, and that its windows were rather close to the ground, as they had been for the past three hundred years. As Percy said as he looked at the cottage, he could prove in court that it had hardly been moving at the time. The only person who seemed to be enjoying the situation was John. He could be seen in his spare time, sweeping up mounds of the chippings and wheeling them in barrowloads to somewhere behind the cottage. When asked what he had in mind for them, he would wink knowingly, and remain silent. As far as I know he never did find a use for them, and I would think that to this very day he is still waiting for some money making idea to strike him.

As the complaints continued, and the council's attitude remained the same, the whole village seethed in anger. Teddy Collins wasn't seen in the village pub for weeks. He said later that he found it best to drop out of sight for a while after a stretch of road had been resurfaced. 'There's no answer to the charges,' he said. 'As long as we use chippings there are going to be breakages, and people are going to blame us.'

Teddy's superior was an arrogant man, not a bit like Teddy himself. As a city dweller he adopted a condescending attitude towards the villagers and what he kept referring to as 'your little problem'. He displayed impatience and lack of tact when he was buttonholed by the locals on one of his visits to Teddy and his gang.

'What are the council going to do about my windscreen?' demanded Percy. Percy had a problem. His car was one that had lost its screen while parked outside the Post Office, and replacements for his nineteen thirty-six model were pretty hard to come by.

'It's nothing to do with me,' said the man. 'If you people would only listen to me and drive more slowly . . .' He was interrupted as Percy uttered one very loud, very rude word and turned away.

It was only a few minutes later, as the man was talking to the gang, that the windscreen of Teddy Collins' council lorry shattered. Teddy's lorry was parked by the side of the road, together with a Land-Rover and his boss's private car. The only thing that was moving on the road at the time was a car that was crawling by in first gear, moving at what was hardly a walking pace. Nevertheless, the windscreen shattered. A few moments later, as a small car was rolling almost noiselessly past in the opposite direction, the council man's hat flew off his head with a jerk. He picked up the bent hat and looked after the car in disbelief. As he did so there was a loud crack and the windscreen of the Land-Rover shattered. The council man blanched. He looked at his own car and then at Teddy Collins. 'I'll be going now, I think,' he said, 'I'm getting out of this place before some lunatic breaks my windscreen.' He climbed into the low-slung model and started the engine. He waited for a solitary cyclist to pass before starting to ease the car out on to the road. The cyclist was no more than a couple of yards past the car when there was another loud crack, and the car's windscreen crazed over in a million tiny cracks. 'Oh no,' groaned the council man as he climbed out of the driving seat.

'Oh dear,' said the cyclist, as he dismounted. It was Percy. 'That's very nasty isn't it?' he said looking concerned. 'Were you going very fast?' The council man didn't answer. Three windscreens in three minutes seemed to him to be a very high score, but as he'd witnessed the breakages with his own eyes he could only put them down to a remarkable coincidence.

While he was removing the broken glass from the front

of his vehicle another car passed down the road at a very reasonable speed. The rear window of the council man's car was drilled by a stone the size of a sparrow's egg. He flung his hat to the ground in despair. 'I thought that I knew all about the problems of loose chippings,' he said through his teeth to Teddy Collins, 'but this kind of thing is absolutely ridiculous.'

Teddy didn't reply, but picked up the man's hat and brushed it with his sleeve before handing it back to him. As he did so he thought to himself that he probably knew quite a bit more than his superior did. He knew for instance that Whistling Jack had lost two windscreens in three days, and that Jack's livelihood depended on his having his van in running order. He also knew of Whistling Jack's almost legendary prowess with a catapult. And he knew for certain that Whistling Jack was that very day working on the roof of the village hall, which was the nearest building to the spot where the three vehicles were standing.

When Len took John on an afternoon's pigeon shooting, it was very much against his better judgement. He had refused to even consider the matter at all when Dolly Foster had first suggested it to him, but Dolly was a distant cousin of Len's, and she wasn't the type to give up easily. Having enlisted the support of every member of the family, she launched a series of attacks, and in the end Len surrendered. 'He might never be the world's greatest shot,' said Dolly, 'but I want him to be able to bring home something for the pot now and then, after we're married, just like any other normal man.'

Len had his own opinion about the difference between John and any other normal man, but he held his tongue for the sake of peace in the family. He checked that John had got himself a current shotgun licence, and then lent him his oldest and least valued gun. Then, with Young 'Enry's full blessing, they set out to wreak havoc among the wood pigeons on Young 'Enry's farm.

Things just didn't go well for John from the outset. He

missed everything that he aimed at, but he did nearly hit Len's dog on two occasions, once even when the dog was walking patiently ten yards behind them. The old dog knew something about John by sheer instinct. Len could tell that by the way that its back went up and its ears went down whenever it looked at him.

Len, on the other hand, hit everything that he aimed at, and did it with such casual ease that John soon became angry. The worse that John's temper got, the worse also did his aim. He raised his gun with a snarl, and fired at a squirrel halfway up a tree. He missed the squirrel completely. He also missed the tree.

It was this shot that Weasel Peters heard as he was tending his snares deeper in the copse. He had already collected a pair of rabbits, and paused with them in his hand as he heard Len and John approaching. He recognized the sound of Len's voice, and his first instinct was to run, as Len had every cause to be annoyed with him, apart from the fact that Weasel was poaching on Len's patch. If Len had been poaching himself it might not have been so bad, but it was obvious from the way that he was striding through the trees that he had permission to shoot on the land.

Weasel decided that the best thing that he could do was to hide and let the two men go past. He climbed up into the thick foliage of a tree and settled himself as deep as he could in the fork of its biggest limbs. He made certain as he did so that he disturbed any birds that were in the trees, as he didn't want the two guns pointing in his direction when the two men went by.

Len and John strolled on through the trees, Len potting the odd bird, John missing the odd dozen. Suddenly, from almost under their feet, a rabbit sprang up and raced away into the undergrowth. Instinctively John pulled the trigger of his gun. Unfortunately, his gun was not pointing at the rabbit at the time, but was being carried at an angle of forty-five degrees from the ground. The shot peppered into the foliage of a tree quite a distance away, sending quite a shower of tattered leaves floating down. Among the leaves there also fell two fat rabbits. Len's jaw dropped. He looked at the rabbits and then at John in disbelief. 'Impossible,' he said, and he squatted down on his haunches, scratching his head. 'It's impossible. He misses every blarsted thing that he aims at, then he shoots two rabbits with one shot, and out of a tree.' He shook his head. 'They'll never believe me when I tell 'em.'

John was as astounded as Len at his success, but he didn't get much time to play the mighty hunter. Weasel's pleading voice came out of the foliage overhead. 'Don't let him shoot again, Len, for goodness sake. Not until I've put at least a couple of miles between him and me.' The slim brown figure wriggled out of the branches and squirmed down the tree. It was easy to see why Weasel had dropped the two rabbits. He was liberally sprinkled with shot, and it was fortunate for him that he had been facing away from John, and had been almost out of range, and had taken most of the pellets in the meatier parts of his body.

Len decided that John had exercised his skills enough for the first day, and called a halt to the shoot, saying that he had better make sure that Weasel got safely back to his own village as soon as possible. John didn't much fancy the prospect of facing Ben and Dolly and admitting that during the course of the whole afternoon he hadn't managed to hit even one pigeon, so he dropped into the pub as soon as it opened, and gulped down a couple of pints of liquid courage. He was about to leave when he was drawn into conversation by a stranger who was also standing at the bar. The man showed great interest in the shooting incident, and John saw no harm in relating the saga to a perfect stranger. By plying John with another two or three swift pints the man managed to get most of the details out of him. 'What were you shooting?' asked the man.

'Rabbits,' said John, after a long moment's pause.

'Rabbits?' asked the stranger, 'Up a tree?'

'I got two,' said John defiantly, 'but Len took them.'

'I think it might be better if I left that bit out altogether,' said the stranger.

'Left it out of what?' asked John.

'Why, the paper,' answered the man. 'I'm a reporter on the local rag, didn't you know?'

And that was how we in the village first got to know of it. It was in the paper the next day, and Weasel never spoke to Len or John for a long time afterwards. Maggie and I hadn't known that Weasel was a family man until we saw the headlines. 'Father of twelve in shooting mishap,' it said. 'Mistaken for a rabbit.'

In every community there are one or two people who would dearly love to run the whole show, if only the other people would give them the chance. They can be found all over, in every walk of life, telling anyone who will listen how they could run their firms, if only the bosses would retire, or how they could run City Hall, or solve the current political crisis. They all have this in common, they are convinced that they are terribly capable and efficient, while the rest of us are not, and they never achieve anything except in their daydreams.

We had two such people in our village, and by a remarkable coincidence they were married to each other. How Mr and Mrs Benjamin kept their faith in their superior talents was a mystery considering the disorganized life that they led. Mr Benjamin worked for a big city firm, and commuted daily. Having on a few rare occasions obliged him by cashing his monthly salary cheque, I knew that his pay was extremely modest, but he reconciled this with his unusual ability by stating regularly that if it wasn't for the fact that the firm would go bankrupt without him, he would leave, and take one of the many very highly paid jobs that he knew he could get if he so wished.

Mrs Benjamin ran the home like a factory. Every single piece of furniture was chosen for its functional qualities alone, colour and shape playing no part in the choice. Her kitchen produced meals that were calculated in the same way that a battery egg producer calculates the diet of his hens. The walls of the kitchen were papered with diet sheets and calorie charts, and these were strictly adhered to. The fact that their three children were the palest, skinniest, and least energetic children in the village school, and that she and her family had skull-like features and ribs that twanged in a high wind was regarded by Mrs Benjamin as proof of the success of her system, and a tribute to her efficiency. The rest of the villagers stated to one another bluntly that she and her husband were barmy, and that it was a shame about the children.

When Mrs Benjamin, who had been trying very hard for a very long time to get on to the Village Hall committee, was allowed to assist in the preparation of the Old Folks' Tea, it wasn't because the committee's high opinion of her abilities. It was because all the other helpers, including the invaluable Miss Money, were indisposed at the same time. Mr Benjamin was politely but firmly refused permission to erect his stereo equipment in the hall, and fill the old folk's ears with music and song. Previous experience with the loudspeaker system on the sports field had led the committee to the conclusion that Mr Benjamin's talents were more suited to the simple manual tasks, and they promised to call on him to help stack the chairs after the tea. He turned quite sullen after this, and said that he had just remembered a previous engagement that clashed with the Old Folk's Tea.

When the day came, and the old folks had been whisked away on their coach outing, Mrs Benjamin's only helper failed to turn up, and she was left, to her secret delight, in full charge. She pottered around in the empty echoing hall, setting out cutlery and crockery, and arranging the chairs and tables in perfectly straight lines. In the kitchen she counted out the plates and started dishing out the tea. It was smoked salmon salad. The pensioners themselves had voted for smoked salmon, and Mrs Benjamin doled it out on to the plates carefully, treating it almost with awe. There were forty-one portions, and the committee had allowed for three ounces of salmon per person. They had provided eight pounds of the delicious fish, which meant that there should have been five ounces over, to allow for any mistakes. After Mrs Benjamin had dealt out on to each plate a portion that she considered to be verging on the extravagant, she still had three and a half pounds of salmon untouched. She counted the plates again. Forty-one. That was right. What had gone wrong then? She checked and double checked, and then decided that someone on the committee had made a mistake. Too much smoked salmon, and at that price! She pursed her thin lips, and shook her thin head. They certainly needed her on that committee, that was obvious. With her doing the organizing, this kind of thing would never happen. People wouldn't listen to her, that was the trouble with this village. She carried on with her work, scraping margarine thinly over slices of bread.

At four o'clock on the dot the coach pulled up again outside the village hall, and the pensioners invaded the dining-room with all the noise and energy of a boy scout troop. The coldish wind had given them a good appetite on their tour of the wildlife park. They each grabbed a chair and were soon seating themselves at tables of their own choice, even moving two tables together so that friends could sit with each other. Attempts by Mrs Benjamin to organize them in neat rows were ignored, and she was told to 'Get to it, Gel, and git up the grub.'

The plates of salad were quickly distributed, and Mrs Benjamin was busy pouring tea into rows of cups when she was distracted by a cluster of faces at the hatchway. 'What's happened to our smoked salmon?' demanded one old lady.

Mrs Benjamin paled. 'What do you mean?' she asked weakly, peering at the plate that was being thrust at her.

The old lady looked round at the other pensioners with raised eyebrows. Then she explained slowly, as if to a simple child. 'We pay for our own Old Folks' Tea,' she said. 'We elect our own committee and decide how much of our own money we will spend. We decided this year to give ourselves a bit of a treat, as we had some money in hand.'

'Yes, that's right,' interrupted Charlie impatiently, 'and we bought eight pounds of best smoked salmon. That's three ounces each and near on half a pound left over. What have you done with it?'

Mrs Benjamin gasped. For a moment she was speechless, and then she found words. 'Three ounces of salmon each?' she said. 'Why, a quarter is enough to make a meal for my family of five people.'

'Your family ain't people,' snapped Charlie. 'They're a bundle of skellingtons. They don't need food like human beings do. Now, what have you done with all our smoked salmon?'

Mrs Benjamin's skinny frame quivered with rage. 'Why you disgusting, greedy old man,' she said. 'Here's your salmon.' And snatching up a dollop of the fish, she pressed it firmly into Charlie's outstretched clawlike hand.

'Why you skinny old faggot,' yelled Charlie, and promptly threw the lump of fish through the hatchway at Mrs Benjamin.

It was most unfortunate that the lady who was supposed to be helping Mrs Benjamin chose that very moment to arrive. She opened the door and walked quickly into the kitchen, and as she did so she intercepted the lump of flying fish with the end of her nose. In one glance she took in Charlie, who had obviously thrown the fish, and the aggressive expression on his wrinkled old face. She was not a timid woman at the best of times, and today, hot and flustered after hurrying, and hours behind with all her work, she was just in the mood to deal with Charlie. She crossed quickly to the hatchway, and leaning through it, caught him firmly by one ear, pulling him towards her. Then she snatched up a handful of salmon and smacked it into his face, sending him reeling backwards. Charlie staggered away and slumped into a chair, and started wiping the mess from his face and glasses in a dazed kind of way.

Those old people who had started eating straight away, instead of arguing about the size of their portions, had by this time cleared their plates, and they arrived in a stream at the hatchway and thrust their plates through at Mrs Benjamin.

'More?' she said, disbelievingly, as she faced the rows of new enemies lined up before her. 'You've each had enough for two already, and that's two normal people, not old folk. You don't need as much to eat as young people do.'

'Don't you tell us what to eat,' she was told, 'we'll eat a pound of salmon each if we feel like it. We pay for it. Now give us some more.' Mrs Benjamin did so, and thumped out the portions with such vigour that the fish was soon all gone, and there were still a number of plates being held out towards her.

When Miss Money, pale and sniffing with her cold, arrived together with the vicar, she was bombarded with complaints as soon as she set foot through the door.

'Not enough salmon.'

'I've not had half an ounce.'

'Who's had all my share?'

'I'm going home to get a bit of tea, I'll starve if I have to last out on what I've just had.' And similar remarks.

In the kitchen, the solitary volunteer was clattering cups and saucers angrily. Mrs Benjamin had left, she said, after causing a riot by giving too much smoked salmon to some people and not enough to others. She'd never seen such a mess in all her life, and that Mrs Benjamin, well, she couldn't run a raffle.

It was when Miss Money was making her little speech of apology to the old folk, and promising that she would make it up to them at some future date, that she noticed old Charlie, Charlie had bits of salmon on his shirt front, and bits on his chin. He had bits on his ears, and even had a large flake of it sitting on top of his bald shiny head. 'There would have been enough salmon for everyone,' said Miss Money sadly, her eyes fixed on Charlie, 'if certain greedy people hadn't taken advantage of the inefficiency of our inexperienced staff.' Her eyes never wavered. 'One or two,' she said, 'must have had far more than their fair share.' There was silence after she had spoken, and her eyes still stayed sadly on old Charlie. So did the eyes of the vicar, but not so sadly, more accusingly. One by one all the other pairs of eyes in the hall swivelled round to stare at the old man.

'Look at him,' said one voice in disgust. 'He's got a bigger piece of salmon on top of his head than I had on my plate.'

Charlie peered round at them all short-sightedly through his smeared spectacles, his face red. 'What's the matter with you all?' he shouted. 'What are you all staring at me for?'

It must be said for Mrs Benjamin that although she went down in history as one of the most inefficient people ever to help out at a village hall function, she gave old Charlie on that day a reputation for greediness that stuck with him for the rest of his life. If that had been her intention from the outset, then she would have been judged to have done it very efficiently indeed.

October gave way to November, and a change came over the countryside. We had the occasional frost in the mornings, and in the evenings owls hooted. The dark nights were here again, and with them came incidents that caused Maggie and me a great deal of amusement and interest. It was in November that the village was to discover that it had a ghost.

EIGHT

NOVEMBER

TEDDY COLLINS was a roadman. He was the foreman in charge of a gang of men that the council employed to keep the roads of the area in good repair. If anyone should consider that a man who earns his living mending roads is an unskilled worker, he should have a talk with Teddy Collins. His knowledge of the different types of road, what foundations were required, what surfacing materials, what drainage for a given situation, was impressive. When the contractors had been involved in the laying of the sewer down the village street, the absence of records had led to the accidental uprooting of drains, water pipes, and even the cable to the telephone kiosk. The man driving the mechanical digger was hardly to blame as the position of these underground obstacles was unknown. Teddy, who had been pasing one day, had pulled up in his lorry and had amazed the engineer in charge by drawing in a matter of minutes, a minutely detailed map of the roads of the village and surrounding area. Every pipe and cable was shown, even some very old unofficial drains that were buried very deeply indeed beneath the road, these latter having been laid long before Teddy had been born, but he knew the exact position of every one. He had refused to divulge the source of his information to the engineer, but it was widely rumoured in the village that the firm had found his information so useful that they had sent Teddy a cheque in gratitude when the job had been completed. I had been as intrigued as the engineer by this demonstration of knowledge, and was quizzing Teddy about it one night as we walked home from the village pub.

'The information is all round us,' said Teddy. 'Most people just aren't interested in roads, so they take no notice, but it's all there if you want to look.'

It was a clear moonlit night and I shivered slightly. 'There'll be a hard frost tomorrow,' I said. 'I can feel it in the air now.'

'Yes,' said Teddy, 'and because of that, right now you could find any old pipe or drain that you wanted to, if you looked for it. Just you have a proper good look at that road there in front of us.'

I looked, and saw what I had never seen before, or if I had seen it hadn't registered at the time. The road ahead was lightly sprinkled with the finest possible covering of frost. The moonlight, reflecting from it, gave it a slightly lighter appearance than usual. All along the road, crossing it in places, running parallel to it in others, there were darker, damper lines, untouched as yet by the frost. These were the lines of every pipe and cable beneath the surface. It was a full scale reproduction of Teddy's map.

When the dark nights came to the village, so did the rustlers. Large vans without lights would draw up at the gateways to remote fields, and several men would leap out and go into action without a word being spoken. Sheep were the favourite target, and these would be quickly rounded up and thrown into the back of the van. After such attacks it was not unusual for injured animals to be found lying in the fields, or wandering the lanes, having escaped through the open gate. For this the rustlers were hated by the countryfolk, whether farmers or not. It was one thing to kill an animal to eat it, but to allow an animal to suffer unnecessarily was inexcusable.

Young 'Enry took to taking his sheep into the stockyard every night, and leaving the lights there burning, so that the flock was always in full view from the farmhouse. The nightly round up meant extra work, and Ben and Shorty were kept busy, as was the young sheepdog that Young 'Enry had bought, but for a while at least, the plan worked, and he lost no sheep to the rustlers.

One night, before he went to bed, Young 'Enry took up his gun and went for a last stroll round the yard. All was peaceful, and he was going back to the house when he heard a sheep. It was a couple of fields away, but he was pretty certain that it was on his land. It was bleating and baaing piteously, and simply couldn't be ignored. Cursing Ben and Shorty, who must have missed the animal on the round up, 'Enry took a lamp and the dog, and set out to find the stray. After a pretty lengthy search the animal was located in the copse on the far side of the farm. It was in the middle of a clump of foliage and was surrounded by branches and bushes that must have been placed there on purpose. It was tethered by a short rope. After loosening the sheep, Young 'Enry wasted a couple of minutes just standing and scratching his head, wondering what was going on. By the time that the truth struck him, it was far too late. He raced back across the fields, the dog racing ahead of him. When he got back, the scene was peaceful. His wife was still soundly asleep in bed, and his sheep were gone.

It was shortly after the night of the rustlers that P.C. Danby gave his talk on 'Security on the modern farm'. The talk was given in the village hall, and as it was free, was attended by most of the villagers. Whether they were farmers or not, it didn't matter, they came to get whatever they could out of the occasion. After about three quarters of an hour of official advice, most of which was read from notes, in a loud flat monotone, Danby sat down, and the floor was open for debate. Charlie started things off nicely by saying that as most farmers made far too much money anyway, sympathy with them over any loss would be a waste of time. 'I just wish that I had a few old sheep to worry about, that's all,' he said.

'I'll sell you a few then, and you can start worrying,' said Young 'Enry.

'I thought that you told the insurance people that all your sheep had been stolen,' said Danby.

'Oh, yes, so they were,' said Young 'Enry, 'I keep forgetting.' 'Enry then appeared to become extremely interested in the next speaker, who was suggesting that each sheep should be fitted with its own individual siren, but Danby sat for quite a long while staring thoughtfully at Young 'Enry.

It was George who suggested a vigilante force. 'Who the devil do you think would be scared of you lot?' John asked.

Several of the older men, stung by this, replied that in the wartime they had been in the home guard, and perhaps they knew a thing or two that John didn't. 'We could take it in turns to stand watch of a night like we did then,' said one old timer. 'We could disguise ourselves as mawkems perhaps.'

John replied that he thought that they were already disguised as mawkems, and very convincingly too. Young 'Enry intervened before blows were struck, and said that it would be pointless for anyone to keep watch on his place, as the damage had already been done, and Danby stated grimly that if anyone took the law into their own hands, he would have them, and that was for sure. He then cleared his throat, and when his serious manner had caught the attention of the audience said that it was true that the insurance company had promised that a reward would be paid for the information that led to the recovery of the sheep. 'Now I'm pretty certain,' he said meaningfully, as he looked round at the sea of faces, 'that even if only a few of the sheep that were reported stolen were found, they would pay out a part of the reward money.' He sat down, but kept his eyes fixed on Young 'Enry. So did most of the people in the hall, except those who nodded and winked to each other, or huddled in small groups with their heads together.

Young 'Enry didn't have a very good night's sleep. His mind was in a turmoil, and he was constantly being disturbed by a series of bangs and creaks around the farm-yard and outbuildings. Dark figures flitted from shed to barn, and someone could easily have been shot if it hadn't been for the fact that Young 'Enry could easily identify each intruder at fifty feet.

At the crack of dawn Young 'Enry rang P.C. Danby. 'It's about my sheep,' said 'Enry.

'Oh yes,' said the sleepy policeman, 'you're a bit earlier than I expected.'

'Some of them have come back,' said Young 'Enry.

'I thought that they might,' yawned Danby.

'Yes,' said 'Enry, 'they wandered back into the field dur-ing the night.' He didn't sound at all pleased at the wan-derers' return. 'They must have been roaming about the fields for the past few days.'

'Yes, they must,' said Danby. 'How many did you say there were?'

'Oh, er, ten, all together,' said Young 'Enry.

'Twelve did you say?' asked Danby. There was a slight pause.

'Oh, er, yes. Twelve,' said 'Enry.

'That's just about the figure I had in mind,' said Danby and put the phone down.

In rural areas ghost stories are commonplace. The absence of street lighting may have something to do with this, but I have always found that country people are more ready to believe in tales of the supernatural than city dwellers.

When the two city folk staggered into the village pub one night and swore that they had just seen a ghost, we were all interested. The two young men said that they had been driving slowly through the village, fog lamp probing the gloom, when they had come to the bridge, which was only a couple of hundred yards from the pub. They were lost, and were relieved when they saw a figure standing at the side of the road. It was a man's figure, they said, and dressed in a cloak of some kind, and was wearing a wide-brimmed hat. The two travellers had stopped the car to ask the way, and the man, so they swore, had disappeared before their eyes. 'There was nowhere that he could have gone,' they said. 'He had to pass us or go into the river.' The two had leapt back into the car and had stopped at the first lights that they had come to, which was the village pub. There was no doubt that the two young men were shaken, and were convinced that they had seen something supernatural, and some of the locals were impressed. A group of young men set out to explore the bridge for themselves, but came back smartly when it was pointed out that they would miss their turn on the dartboard if they went outside.

By the time that the reporters arrived on the scene, the story had developed as it passed from mouth to mouth. The car had been halted, it was now said, by an apparition in the middle of the road, with uplifted hand. The car's engine had mysteriously cut out, and the apparition had only disappeared when the driver had tried to touch it. One reporter managed to add a bit to the story himself. He found an old churchyard that was not too far away from the bridge, and he found a couple of elderly villagers who would be prepared to say that it was not impossible that the building of the bridge had in some way interfered with the peace and tranquillity of the old graves. Photographs for the press were taken in the bar, and the likenesses of Whistling Jack with his pursed up lips, Buddy, with his awful gleaming teeth, old Charlie, with his gleaming bald head, and Shorty Smith staring morosely into the camera, appeared in the local papers. In one picture, Buddy, sitting in a gloomy corner, had almost disappeared from view, but like Alice's cat, the smile alone remained behind.

A courting couple next reported seeing the ghost, and used it as an excuse for being home late. Then there was a tramp, who drank freely for a week on his tale, until one night he overdid things by swearing that the figure bore a striking resemblance to Adolf Hitler.

It was on another dark and foggy night that I saw the

ghost for myself. I was walking over the bridge towards the pub, after calling on a friend, and I paused when I heard the snuffling and snorting of a coypu in the river below. I slowly became aware, as I stood there, that there was another figure standing at the other end of the bridge. It was a dim shape at that distance, but I thought that I could make out that it was wearing a hat with a turned down brim and its trousers tucked into knee boots, or perhaps Wellingtons. I was standing as still as I could, and trying to make out more of the figure, when it disappeared from my view, almost as if the earth had swallowed it up. I crossed the bridge as quickly and as quietly as I could to the spot where I had last seen the figure standing. There was only one place that it could possibly have gone, and that was into the river. Whoever it was who had been standing there, he must have jumped down the bank to the water's edge. I looked down, and saw the man below as the fog thinned for a second. He waded into the water, quietly, and made far less noise about it than the coypu had done. The water here was only about two feet deep, and the man waded into the middle of the stream, and then turned. He disappeared under the bridge. I crossed the road on tiptoe and waited for him to reappear. When he did so I could only just make him out in the fog. He went to the right hand bank and climbed slowly and quietly out of the water. He paused then for quite a long time, looking slowly around him, and I began to think that he had seen me, however, he turned and ducked through the barbed wire fence that protected the thicket that was at that point bounded by the river. The thicket was owned by Lady Blanche, and her gamekeeper was known to be a very nasty customer to cross. He also kept a couple of equally nasty dogs, and it was his boast that he could use his dogs to track down a poacher by smell alone, hours after they had passed that way. By entering and leaving the thicket by this way, the man had at least avoided that particular means of detection, and I had to admire his tenacity. In spite of the poor visibility and his unusual dress, I had recognized the ghost. The way that he had ducked through that wire had been unmistakable. It was Len.

As I walked home I realized that I was one of the only two people who knew the truth about the ghost of the bridge. I decided to keep the knowledge to myself. It was only a matter of time, I told myself, before the ghost was laid for good, either by Lady Blanche's gamekeeper, or by P.C. Danby, or by sheer bad luck. But I was mistaken. The ghost was never caught, and the legend grew with time. The last time that the tale was told to me, by an earnest young university student, who was under the impression that because I didn't have a Norfolk accent I was a visitor, the ghost had multiplied into three or four figures, each dressed like a monk, and shining with an unearthly light. They were said to hold up the traffic on certain days of the year, and always made their exit by walking away on top of the water. When I asked whether anyone had ever tried to track down the ghosts with dogs, I was laughed at. Everyone knows, I was told, that dogs cannot track ghosts. 'Len,' I thought to myself, 'you've hit on a pretty good cover, even if it did come about by accident.'

The pavement outside the Post Office was inset with concrete slabs that had slots in them. The purpose of these slots was to take the front wheel of a cycle when it was being parked. Nearly everyone in the village had a bicycle, whether they had a car or not. Even Dr John left his new car in the garage for a couple of days every week and toured the village on two wheels. The vicar was hardly ever seen in his car, and his wife never was. She would ride slowly along the country lanes on an elderly upright machine that required such a rigid posture that she looked positively regal.

The parking slots were in daily use, and often full. Sometimes a cycle would be forgotten and left there all night, and the small boys of the village would often look through the door to see who was in the shop, and if there was a bike outside who's owner couldn't be seen, they would ride it along to the owner's house and hope to get a free ride and some small reward into the bargain. We had to put a stop to this after a couple of irate housewives had to walk home with their shopping after being missed in the shop by the boys. Sometimes a cycle would be damaged while parked in the slots. This would happen if the bike was pushed over, the lower part of the wheel, being held in the slots, couldn't move, and the wheel would bend. When this happened the unlucky owner would call on us for help. The nearest garage, which was in the next village, did a good trade in cycle spares, and it was quite common for Maggie and I to be asked to ring them up and ask them if they had a wheel of such and such a size.

Pipes, who had a way with mechanical things, decided to cash in on the local demand, and set himself up in a cycle repairing business. He gave up his afternoon work at the breeze block yard and worked at the business part time at first. He still did his postman's round every morning. His garden shed was soon bulging at the seams, and he was forced to rent bigger premises. Soon he found himself so busy that he gave up his postman's round. His timing was perfect, for shortly afterwards a rise in the price of petrol made cycles very much sought after. People came out from the city to buy his reconditioned machines, and he turned part of his new premises into a small showroom.

Maggie and I were delighted to see Pipes getting on so well, and so were the villagers as a whole. John was the exception. He grumbled that Pipes had beaten him to the draw, that he would have started just such a business, and that it was just a case of bad timing. When someone put it to him that he had never been heard to mention the cycle business John was indignant. 'So what,' he said. 'I would have got round to it, after I'd tried out all the other good business ideas that I keep getting.'

After the first scare caused by the petrol price, people settled back to normal. Everyone who had ever wanted a bike had now bought one, and Pipes found that sales dropped from their frantic peak to a very steady norm. Repairs too had slowed down. Old machines that had been dragged out and reconditioned in the heat of the moment were now hung back on the outhouse wall, awaiting the next crisis. Pipes wasn't kept very busy. He reluctantly applied for his postman's round again and was immediately accepted by the Post Office. Not very long afterwards, he offered to sell the business to John.

'Business,' sneered John, 'What business? I'll bet you don't take enough in a week to keep me in beer.' He laughed at the thought. 'Your business is bust and you know it. I could have told you that from the start, if that idea had been any good at all, I'd have thought of it a long time before you did.'

'Well, make me an offer for the stock then,' said Pipes.

'Stock,' scoffed John. 'What stock? You might get a scrap man to take them off your hands if you tip him.'

Pipes packed up the business altogether, and went back to his other part time job at the breeze block makers.

A couple of weeks later, an advert appeared under a box number in the local paper. It said that a collector was interested in purchasing any old bicycles that were in going order and over thirty years old. The advert caught John's eye. Pipes and his stock! John cursed himself for a fool. Fancy missing the chance of buying up all those old bikes that Pipes had offered to sell him. Why hadn't he thought of collectors at the time.

When Pipes finished work, he found John waiting for him. 'I'll just walk along home with you if you don't mind,' he said. 'I'd like to have a quick look at those old bikes that you've got. You never know, there might be something there that I can do something with, if the price is right.'

'Have a look then,' said Pipes. 'They're all still for sale, but I'm not giving them away.'

The outhouse at Pipes' home was crammed with old bikes. There was a heap of them, a tangle of them. When they had sorted them out they counted sixteen in going order, and the haggling began. John found that his task was harder than he had expected it to be. He started out by saying that he would take the lot off Pipes' hands if he would accept ten pounds for them. Pipes wouldn't, and almost an hour later John parted with the sum of eighteen pounds, plus one ladder and one wheelbarrow, and a portable hen house that he was buying on hire purchase. He had gone far higher than he had intended, but he was still quite confident that he could make a good profit out of the deal. It was late into the evening when John made his last trip to Pipes' home and collected the last two bikes. He couldn't resist the opportunity to gloat, and he pulled the local paper from his pocket. 'Here,' he said, triumph in his tone, 'have a look at that.'

Pipes took the paper. The advert was underlined. 'I shouldn't bother answering this if I were you,' he said calmly. 'I thought that I would start collecting, that's why I put the advert in, but I changed my mind when you made me such a good one. Mind you, it was worth my while. I only gave a couple of pounds for five of them old bikes this morning.'

When Charlie won the transistor radio in the raffle, it was presented to him in the village pub. Charlie, whose own radio was an ancient thing half the size of a tea chest that had served him faithfully for twenty odd years, looked at the new fangled thing with deep distrust. He turned the switch, and a Beethoven symphony rang tinnily through the bar. 'That's classical,' said Percy knowledgeably. Percy had once owned a record of Paul Robeson singing something from an opera that was far too highbrow for his liking.

'Will this thing give me the weather forecasts?' asked Charlie dubiously.

'It'll give you the same as your old set does,' said George. 'Give it here.' He took the radio and showed Charlie how to operate it. Charlie wasn't impressed. When George got round to showing him where the batteries went, Charlie interrupted.

'Do you mean that I've got to go on buying them things

for ever more?' he asked. 'A proper white elephant, that's what that is.'

John, who had been sitting quietly but eyeing the radio greedily, butted in. 'I'll give you a pound for it if you don't want it,' he said.

'Five pounds more like,' said Charlie. They haggled for a short time, then agreed on three pounds, and John took his radio.

He hadn't had the radio in his possession more than ten minutes when it stopped working, and no amount of twiddling with the knobs or shaking the thing would make it work again. 'Charlie, I want my money back,' he demanded, pushing the radio towards the old man.

'You won't get it,' said Charlie, pushing it back again. 'You bought the radio just as it was, and it was going all right.'

'Well what about the guarantee?' asked John. 'A new radio should have a guarantee with it like anything else that's new. If you didn't get a guarantee with it then you were robbed.'

That was different. Charlie didn't mind John being robbed, but he did mind very much being robbed himself. He turned on George. 'Here, where's my guarantee?'

George scratched his head uncomfortably, and tried to explain. It was he who had donated the radio to the Village Hall committee as a prize. It was new all right, George having won it himself in a previous raffle, but he hadn't liked the tone of it, and had generously handed it back to be raffled again. The guarantee, however, had been filled in and sent off in his name, and was non-transferable.

'Well then,' said John, 'you send it back and have it fixed.'

'No fear,' said George, 'I gave it away and don't want anything more to do with it. It isn't mine anymore.' He paused and a thought struck him. 'Anyway,' he said, 'who would pay for the postage?'

'He would,' said John, pointing at Charlie.

'He wouldn't,' said Charlie emphatically. 'It's your radio not mine.'

'Yes, but I bought a new radio, not an old broken one,' shouted John.

'You didn't,' said Charlie, 'you bought a second-hand one.'

'Third hand,' said a man at the other end of the room.

'In future,' said George nastily to the room in general, 'I'll take my radio, or anything else that I don't want, and smash it up and throw it in the dustbin. It'll save a lot of trouble.'

'I think that he should sort it out,' said Charlie to John, looking at George. 'After all he started it.'

'Tell you what I'll do,' said George through set teeth. 'I'll give you the price of your raffle ticket, and I'll take that blarsted radio and jump up and down on it.'

'What,' bellowed John, 'after I've given him three pounds for it?'

George turned to Charlie. 'Will you give him his three pounds back?'

'I will not,' said Charlie. 'I won a prize in the raffle. The three pounds is mine.' And so the argument went on.

The door quietly opened, and Miss Money peeped coyly in. 'Ah gentlemen,' she said, noting that there was a lull in the conversation. 'We are having a raffle in aid of the church building fund. I wonder if I can interest you in a few tickets?'

A few moments later she was outside again, her cheeks scarlet. The men in the bar, so well known to her and usually so polite, had shocked her by unanimously suggesting a course of action regarding her tickets that sounded excruciatingly painful, if not physically impossible. 'I simply can't understand it,' she muttered to herself as she hurried away, 'they surely must have had an awful lot to drink.'

When the solicitor held a barbecue at White Bungalow one bright and breezy Saturday, the whole village knew about it. The well trimmed lawns were set out with rustic benches and tables, and there was a bar. We were experiencing a dry spell of weather and the afternoon was quite warm. As the function got under way the smell of thick steaks being grilled over charcoal drifted across the village. It was a most exclusive affair, and though the villagers might gaze enviously through the gates, their chances of gaining entry were precisely nil. It did not surprise me, therefore, that when I asked John if he would care to do me a favour and run up to White Bungalow with an order, he almost fell over himself in his eagerness. The solicitor had phoned, saying that they were running out of charcoal and could I supply some? I had told him that I didn't keep much on stock, there not being a great demand for that kind of thing in the village, but that I would send along whatever I could find. It was while I was ringing round the nearby village stores that I learned that there was a shortage of charcoal. We actually imported tons of the stuff from the continent. I was amazed. Fairy tales from childhood sprang to mind, where the English forests were always deep and dark, with charcoal burners every few yards. The thought of some foreign charcoal burner waxing fat on the profit from our barbecues annoyed me intensely. Why on earth couldn't we burn our own charcoal?

I was in this frame of mind when John returned from his delivery to White Bungalow. He was brimming over with enthusiasm for the house, the guests, and their life style. 'You know, that's the only way to live,' he kept saying, a dazed look in his eyes. 'Make money, and then more money, and then some more again.'

I then casually mentioned that if a man wanted to make himself a little money he might do worse than go in for charcoal burning. I told him about the imports, and the shortage. I also mentioned the high price that the stuff was being sold for. John's eyes gleamed. I realized a while later that I had allowed myself to become carried away, and that it was only too easy to start John off on some wild goose chase, but there was nothing that I could do about it by then. He had the bit firmly between his teeth.

John went about the village for days, chatting to the old men, trying to find anyone who knew anything about charcoal burning. He didn't meet with very much success, the skill having apparently died out with the men who practised it. In the end he was forced to turn to old Charlie, who became his main source of information. Charlie had never been a charcoal burner himself, but said that as a boy he had seen the operation performed many times. Slowly, over pint after pint of beer, he released his scant information to the eager John. 'First you've got to prepare your hearth,' he said. 'Make it as big as you think you'll need and make it dead flat.' He drained his glass and sat silent until a refill was placed before him. 'All the stones have to be removed,' he said, 'cos they explode when they get hot, and the ground's going to get very hot before you've done.' John scribbled hasty notes round the edges of beer mats as Charlie spoke. 'Then you pile your wood up,' he said. 'Any old wood will do. Branches, or offcuts from a joiner's shop. Hardwoods are best, but you won't be able to get enough of them, so I should use anything you can lay your hands on.'

'It all sounds very easy,' said John doubtfully.

'It is easy,' snapped Charlie. 'If it wasn't easy you wouldn't be able to do it, so shut up and listen. John shut up. 'As I said,' went on Charlie, 'you pile all your wood up neat like, like a haystack, with no gaps in if you can manage it. Then you cover the whole pile with straw. You try and make it as airtight as possible.'

'But if it's airtight it won't burn, will it?' asked John.

Charlie glared at him. 'Just one more of your silly remarks and I'll go off and have a game of dominoes.' John licked the end of his pencil and kept quiet. 'Then cover the whole heap with a couple of inches of mould,' said Charlie. (When a Norfolk man uses the word mould he usually means soil.) 'You build the pile round a great stovepipe, to act as a chimney,' said Charlie, suddenly remembering. 'A four inch one should be about right, sloping right down into the middle. When you've finished you stick your fire down the pipe to get it going. A drop of paraffin might help, but not too much or you'll get a heap of white ash instead of black charcoal.' The crowd in the bar were by this time as deeply interested in the instructions as John was, this being one of the few rural skills that they were not all adept at.

Charlie warmed to the task, racking his brains for details. 'Once you've got it lit,' he said, 'you block up the pipe with a lump of clay, and you go away and leave it.' There was silence in the bar.

'What then?' asked John.

'Er, nothing,' said Charlie, hesitantly. 'After about two days and two nights you've got yourself a great heap of charcoal.'

'You sure?' asked John. 'It all sounds very easy.'

Charlie looked round the bar with a scowl. 'If it sounded hard I'd be wasting my time with you, wouldn't I? As it is, I've no doubt that you'll find some way of making a muck up of it.'

John opened his mouth to reply, but changed his mind. Instead he reached over and picked up what was left of the last pint that he had bought Charlie. He drained it at a gulp and strode out before Charlie had time to think of a suitable remark.

When Young 'Enry granted John permission to carry out his charcoal burning on his land, the villagers were puzzled. When it was known that he had told John that he could use as much wood as he required, they were perplexed. They smelt a rat, the whole village did, except John.

John set to work with all the enthusiasm that he showed for any new venture. He worked late for days preparing things as per Charlie's instructions. By Friday night he had constructed something that looked rather like a haystack that had been trodden on, and before he left for bed he encased it in smooth damp earth. Early on the Saturday morning, he lit it. He spent a long time making sure that the pile was burning deep down inside, then he blocked up the pipe and waited. There was nothing at all to do, and no company there among the trees, not that he would have wanted anyone around to share his new found skills. After his strenuous exertions he found the boredom intolerable. He sat for a while, contemplating his wealthy future, and when he got tired of that he went for a walk around the heap. Nothing had changed. There was no smoke, no heat. No sign at all that there was anything going on deep inside. He read and re-read the week old newspaper that he had brought in his lunchbag, and by midday was thoroughly fed up. The afternoon passed terribly slowly, and by tea time he was frantic. He looked at the old newspaper again, and tried to do the crossword. He couldn't. At six he was thinking about the bar in the village pub, the lights, the company. At half past he thought he could hear the sounds of distant revelry ringing over the darkened fields. At seven he could stand it no longer. Telling himself that the pile was certain to be all right, he set off briskly over the fields towards the pub. Once there he fell in with a crowd of his friends, and took pint after pint off them easily by tearing telephone directories in half, and breaking in two the odd six inch nail. At closing time, full of best bitter, he fumbled his way back to Ben's cottage, and slept like a baby, with never a thought for the great fuming mound in Young 'Enry's copse.

Young 'Enry himself had given the mound a great deal of thought. He would have loved to have felled all the trees in the copse long ago, and cultivated that corner of land, but he was not allowed to do so. His father had made quite certain in his will that Young 'Enry would have to leave that corner of the land as sanctuary for wildlife. 'Enry was of the opinion that the copse gave shelter to vermin and poachers, and had come to the conclusion that the only way to clear the land and make it profitable would be for some accident to happen, something which didn't involve him at all, something perhaps like a great fire in the middle of the night.

Young 'Enry crept into the copse before he went to bed. He wasn't surprised to find that John had left, in spite of his good intentions, in fact 'Enry had been relying on just that. He examined the mound, and was impressed by the care that John had taken in building it. A breeze had sprung up, blowing flecks of dried earth from the top of the mound, and

Young 'Enry shivered slightly, but he also smiled. A few minutes later, when he left the copse, some of the carefully placed soil and straw was missing from the mound, and the stovepipe chimney was unblocked. A strong draught was rushing up the pipe, causing a deep roaring sound in the centre of the pile. Instead of gently smouldering, small flames could be seen flickering in the woodpile. Taking a last look from his bedroom, Young 'Enry could see a huge red glow, and sparks flying in the trees. He went to sleep with a smile on his face.

When John went along on Sunday morning to inspect his precious pile of charcoal, all that was left was a heap of white ash. About two thirds of all the trees in the copse had been destroyed in the blaze, but Young 'Enry was very understanding, even sympathetic about the whole thing. He told John that it wasn't his fault, that accidents would happen, and that John was welcome to repeat his attempts at any time. John felt that 'Enry was getting at him in some way whenever he spoke in this manner, but he couldn't quite see how. He grew heartily sick of being asked by the villagers what had gone wrong. He blamed everything on the strong wind that had sprung up, and the fact that he might have had the stovepipe at the wrong angle. It was after the charred stumps had been hauled out and the land ploughed that Young 'Enry added the final touch to John's humiliation. They met up in the pub one night, and the talk inevitably got round to the charcoal business.

'By the way,' Young 'Enry said, 'After I'd got everything sorted out, I ended up with loads and loads of charcoal. All of them charred stumps and things you know. You don't know anyone who wants the stuff do you?' John choked on his beer and the back of his neck went red, but he didn't reply.

The next few weeks were busy for Maggie and me. December was drawing near, and people were thinking of Christmas already. We slipped out of November and into December without hardly noticing.

NINE

DECEMBER

WHEN the village schoolmistress hit on the idea of holding a fifty-fifty sale in order to boost the school fund, she hit on a winner. Every able-bodied person in the village turned up, and the sale was such a huge success that she was begged to make it a regular thing. The idea was to auction any article for the highest possible price. Half of the price obtained went to the owner of the article, and half to the school fund. The schoolteacher numbered all the articles and checked them carefully a hundred times. Then she left the auction itself to her volunteers. The auctioneer was that perpetual volunteer, Mr Benjamin. He attempted to open the proceedings by making a speech, but was shouted down by the crowd, with calls of 'Git on with it, bor', and 'Shut up or push off'. Things were soon swinging along in fine style, the bids flowing in spite of Mr Benjamin. Maggie and I had sent an old worn out typewriter to be auctioned, and on the strength of what that brought had successfully bid for quite a decent bicycle. John, who had his eye on one or two items that he considered bargains, tried to ingratiate himself with the auctioneer. He nodded affably at Mr Benjamin, probably the first person who had done so for a very long time, and found himself the reluctant owner of a tea chest containing three Wellington boots, a war-time gas-mask, and a motor cyclist's crash helmet with a swastika painted on it.

Percy and Charlie had bought between them a half roll of wire netting and were providing unintended entertainment for the crowd of onlookers as they tried to divide it equally in two, helped by two or three barking dogs.

When Mr Benjamin came to the furniture, the crowd pressed forward. There were bargains to be had, and the bidding for the smaller items such as stools and chairs was brisk. At last they came to the sideboard that more than one person had been waiting for. It was a nice looking piece of furniture, but I knew something about it that the crowd didn't. I examined it earlier that day, and had found it to be riddled with woodworm. I had also watched Charlie, its owner, fill all the holes with plasticine, and then wipe the surface over with a handful of brown boot polish. As a piece of furniture I doubted whether the sideboard was worth as much as the price of a pint of beer.

'Now here we have a sideboard,' said Mr Benjamin, revelling in his work. 'Can we have it out in the open please.' His helpers, two young farmworkers, picked up the sideboard and carried it a few yards away from the wall. As they did so, from inside the sideboard came the chink-chinking of coins. The crowd pricked up its ears. One of the young helpers looked at the sideboard with a worried frown. He had examined it earlier, and was certain that the drawers were empty, but he checked again. He pulled out first one drawer and then the other. He found nothing. The crowd was watching him to a man. Mr Benjamin was prattling away to himself. The bidding started, and the crowd showed their interest. As they called out their bids, one against the other, the young man was still examining the sideboard. He lifted one end of it about a foot above the ground. Once again the chinking sound was heard. He lowered it back down again, and the sound was heard again.

I doubt whether there was anyone over the age of thirty in the crowd who didn't remember that type of sideboard well, and knew that the central decorated panel was in fact a concealed cutlery drawer. I also doubt whether there was one person bidding who didn't think that he alone knew the secret, and that the drawer in the sideboard that was being auctioned was filled with coins, perhaps sovereigns. The bidding went wild, and Mr Benjamin went pale. He didn't know what on earth was going on, and he didn't like anything to be going on unless he knew all about it. Some men in the crowd found that their own wives had bid against them in the confusion, and other wives produced money that had been saved up secretly, and handed it over to their husbands, in order to bolster their bids. In the end the sideboard was knocked down to Young 'Enry, who had got as much carried away as the rest of the bidders. He paid more for the old piece than he would have had to pay for a brand new sideboard.

He paid over the cash to the tireless Miss Money, and was pushing his way through the crowd, his fingers itching to get to the drawer, when old Charlie caught him by the arm. 'I see you bought my old sideboard,' he said, grinning up at Young 'Enry.

'Your sideboard?' asked 'Enry, his stomach sinking.

'Yes,' said Charlie. 'Picked it up at a sale, dirt cheap, but I didn't like the look of it once I'd got it home. Still, it'll do for you though, I dare say.' Young 'Enry gritted his teeth and wished to himself that Charlie was a younger man, so that he could stuff him into the blasted sideboard. 'There's just one thing,' said Charlie, his face wrinkled with pleasure as he spoke, 'there's a few washers missing from behind the handles. If you was thinking of doing it up like, making a good job of it, then you'll find a whole collection of washers in the middle drawer.' He cackled at Young 'Enry. 'You know the one I mean,' he said, 'the one that's hidden behind that bit of carving.'

Against my better judgement I allowed myself to be persuaded to attend the first performance of a play that was being performed by the local amateur dramatic society. Maggie had a small part in the play, and nagged me into going along. Knowing most of the cast socially, I didn't relish the idea of sitting for a couple of hours watching them do something that I honestly thought was beyond their capabilities, but as I was told that almost all the men of the village would be there, I agreed to attend. It wasn't that I have anything against amateur actors, but the play that they had chosen to perform was a most difficult one, and I felt sure that they would regret their choice later.

The play was set in a northern mining village, and the characters were supposed to have strong northern accents. Maggie, who with teeth blacked out was playing the part of an evil old crone, did passably well. This was not surprising, since we came from the north, and had relatives who did live and work in such a mining village. The rest of the cast displayed unsuspected depths of imagination as they adopted their stage voices. The females of the cast, each one large and fat, spoke in a tongue that was something in between Liverpool Irish and in inebriated Geordie. The male members of the troupe demonstrated their individuality by speaking in accents that ranged from that of a Devonshire man with a speech impediment to that of a mentally retarded Lowland Scot.

The play was allegedly a drama, but it gave more amusement to the majority of the audience than any farce could have done. The vicar spent the whole of the evening slumped down as low as he could get in his seat, silent tears streaming down his crimson face. Dr John, his eyes unnaturally bright, kept a large handkerchief over the lower part of his face during the whole performance. The solicitor, who arrived late and had obviously had a drink or two, gave vent to a series of high-pitched giggles that at times bordered on the hysterical. The two farmers who were sitting on either side of me simply guffawed loudly, slapping their thighs and shouting 'Gaw help me.'

I bit on my tongue until it hurt, trying desperately to keep a straight face and not hurt Maggie's feelings, but in the end my feelings got the better of me and I was forced to laugh aloud.

The final scene was set in the home of one of the miners, and the actors, playing the part of men who had just finished a day's work at the coal face, had enthusiastically blacked

their faces, until they looked not like miners, but like members of a commando squad setting out on some dangerous mission. The scene had hardly got started when the lighting, which was under the care of Whistling Jack, developed a fault. The stage gradually darkened, and the players took on the appearance of a minstrel troupe, with large white eyes and mouths, the rest of their faces being invisible. Whistling Jack, improvising with remarkable speed, turned on a spotlight. The effect of this as it swung from one miner to another was to illuminate an endless procession of Al Jolsons, each with his eyes closed against the light, while behind him weaved a host of dark figures, stumbling and whispering. The actors lost their places, and the prompter couldn't see his lines. The whispers on and off stage grew louder, and the spotlight panicked and flitted from face to face with dazzling speed. One player was so overcome with embarrassment that he crept under the table to hide, but the ever roving spotlight sought him out and revealed him to the audience for the coward that he was. He shuffled around so as to present his back to the audience, and as he did so one of the fat women trod on his fingers. The crowd cheered. At the back of the stage was a coffin, supposedly holding the body of a dead miner. After a few minutes of darkness and confusion, the body sat up to see what was going on. Immediately the spotlight seized him, and held him for a full half minute, sitting bolt upright and staring petrified at the audience. Then one of the footlights started to smoke. This was too much, and the whispered cry of 'Curtain' was heard.

Whoever it was who talked the group into allowing John to help behind the scenes I do not know, but must assume that it was a jealous member of a rival amateur dramatic group. Groping around in the dark, and striking matches until he ran out of them, John attempted to drop the curtain on the proceedings. All that he managed to do, however, was to lower a backdrop instead. The scene of the miner's cottage was instantly transformed into that of a battleship ploughing through endless seas, with a table, four chairs, and a coffin placed on deck, and the crew of fat ladies and minstrels being raked by harsh rays of an enemy searchlight. A couple of members of the cast had been caught behind the backdrop, and as they made their escape off stage they caused the waves to roll in a most realistic manner in the poor light. Someone stumbled into the trestles that supported the coffin, and one end, the head, crashed to the stage. The roving spotlight zoomed in eagerly, and the audience, who had already seen the corpse sitting up and in perfect health, were now treated to a view of his lower limbs sticking up out of the coffin and performing what looked like cycling exercises. As long as the spotlight held him the other players were reluctant to offer their assistance or even go near the poor man. The leg movements grew weaker as the man slid steadily to the top of the coffin until he was cramped up like a sleeping dormouse and just as still. The curtain finally came jerking down, and the audience applauded wildly, with shouts of 'More, more.'

In the pub later, in a post mortem on the play, Charlie voiced the opinion that it had been excellent. 'The point was,' he explained to a fascinated crowd, 'that there fellow wasn't really dead. They'd have buried him though, if he hadn't kicked up such a struggle at the end. It's a point to watch when you're getting towards the end of the road. I'll certainly watch out when I get old.' He adopted his most aggressive expression. 'Nobody's going to bury me without a struggle.'

As to the individual performances, the compliments flew thick and fast. The greater the difference between the speaking voice of the man on the stage and the man the audience knew him to be, the greater the performance was judged to be. Thus one actor who had been almost unrecognizable beneath his black paint, and who had never got the chance to speak a word, was hailed as a positive genius. 'They could all teach them London actors a thing or two,' I was assured by the two farmers that I had sat next to. 'All except your wife, I'm afraid. If you don't mind me saying so, she couldn't get the accent right. She just doesn't know what them miners really talk like.'

When John started pasting posters up all around the village, people jeered. After they had read the posters though, they stopped jeering and began to show interest. The posters advertised a carpet sale that was to be held in the village hall on the coming Friday, and some of the prices quoted as examples seemed to be very reasonable indeed. When asked why he was working so hard to advertise the sale John replied that as he was a partner in the firm it was in his own interests to advertise it as well as he could. He explained that he and his new found partner had some very big plans for the future, and that small village sales such as the one that they were about to hold in our village, would be dropped in favour of big city operations. 'This is only the start,' said John, 'just see to which lines are more popular with the general public. That's you lot,' he added, in case we didn't understand.

When Friday evening came around, the sale attracted most people from the village, and quite a crowd from the surrounding area. John worked like a horse. He never had a single moment's rest, lugging all the carpets around, and jumping to it at the salesman's every word. They worked very well as a team, but the salesman never did any of the heavy work, and John never handled any of the money. His partner seemed to know all that there was to know about carpets, and had the gift of being able to talk non-stop about the goods that were for sale, even rattling away while giving change to customers, or adding up in his head. Some of the larger carpets, and all of those going to outlying areas, were to be delivered, and John, whenever he got a second's rest from heaving the things about, was kept busy writing addresses down, and giving receipts for the money his partner had taken. A farmer's wife who had been one of the first to buy a small carpet had taken it home herself and then returned to the hall. She told all and sundry that she and her husband were delighted with the purchase. 'Beautiful, it looks,' she said. 'It's that green one over there. Less than half the price I would have had to pay in the city. I don't know how they do it.'

A middle-aged couple who had been wavering uncertainly round the salesman were so impressed by this obviously unsolicited testimonial that they made up their minds and handed over the money for a couple of four by three squares of the same carpet. John scribbled a receipt for them, and his partner took the money.

By around nine thirty the crowd had bought up every bit of carpet on show, and they were still ordering. When two families who each wished to take their purchases with them started arguing about that last piece of red Axminster, the salesman stepped in between them. 'Just a moment friends,' he said, 'there's no need to get excited, we're not going to disappoint anyone. If you'll just wait a moment I'll go to the van and bring some more stock. Everyone will be served, just bear with me for a while.'

John was too busy at the far side of the hall to help his partner with the lifting, but he didn't seem to mind. He nipped smartly out of the door, and left John, perspiring freely, scribbling down the addresses of a whole horde of customers. It was at least ten minutes before he completed his lists and looked round for his colleague, and fifteen minutes before he had become alarmed enough to dash outside himself. The man was gone. So was the van.

When the news was broken to the crowd of people back in the hall near riot broke out. 'You'd better deliver my two bits of that green stuff first of all, or else,' said one farmer threateningly to John.

'How can I?' he pleaded. 'That bit is all that there is.' He pointed to the piece that the salesman had been using as a sample.

'This bit's mine,' said a little dumpy woman, and to emphasize her point she sat down heavily on it, her arms folded.

As Miss Money explained later, she felt that she had to call the police, if only to save John from being tarred and feathered or worse. In the next few days more details of the salesman's activities came to light. His van was found abandoned. It had been hired, and paid for with a cheque that bounced. He had left his hotel without paying his bill, and he owed money for the hire of the village hall. The Village Hall committee made it very plain to John that they expected him to settle that account, if none of the others. The salesman was certain to appear in court, if he was ever found, and for a time it looked as though John might be charged too. 'If I were you I should plead guilty but insane,' said Ben to his son. 'They're bound to believe you.'

As time went by the defrauded customers became even more enraged by the fact that the police had taken no action against John. They wanted to see someone pay for the crime, and as the salesman wasn't to hand they saw no reason why John shouldn't be punished for the two of them. There wasn't much that they could do about the situation except grumble amongst themselves and slander John, but they did stop speaking to him. If he called in for a drink at least half the regulars would turn their backs on him, and at work things were just as bad. When some of us said that we felt sorry for him we were told, even by Ben, that it served him right. John did pay off the debt for the hire of the hall, but as he said many times, he couldn't possibly pay off all the debts, and after all, he had been robbed too. His words fell on deaf ears.

Some weeks later John placed a postcard advert in the Post Office window. It advertised a bicycle for sale. A prospective purchaser showed interest in it, and after examining it, started the inevitable discussion about price. They eventually agreed on the sum of ten pounds as being a fair price for the machine, and they shook hands on it. The man then handed John a slip of paper.

'What's this?' he asked.

'It's a receipt, signed by you, for ten and half quid,' said the man. 'You can keep the change.'

'But I haven't got the money,' protested John.

'No, and I haven't got my carpet,' said the man as he pedalled away.

It was almost closing time on Christmas Eve, and the rush seemed to be over. I had just been congratulating myself on the increase in the sale of boiled ham when I discovered that Mrs Finch had been weighing it out at twenty-five pence per pound instead of twenty-five pence per quarter. 'Still,' I told myself, 'it is Christmas after all. Better forget it.' I had bolted the door and was dimming the lights when there came a roar from outside. I drew back the bolt and was pushed aside as the man threw his weight against the door.

'Why the devil don't you buy yourself a decent clock?'

he demanded angrily. 'One day you close up half an hour late, the next day half an hour early.'

I pointed out politely that the notice on the door stated that we closed at five forty-five, and that it was usually nearer six by the time that I had locked the door.

'Squit!' he said rudely. 'It's only nearing half past now, and you were locking up.'

I stepped behind the counter and switched on the radio that I kept there. The Greenwich time signal for six o'clock was just pipping. 'It's six, I'm afraid,' I said as politely as I could.

'Squit!' he said again, and hauled from his pocket the largest, oldest turnip watch that I had ever seen. 'You can't even rely on the BBC nowadays,' he complained. He held the watch up so that I could see it. It only had one hand, and that one was bent. 'They're half an hour fast tonight,' he said, 'and last night they were half an hour slow.'

On Christmas Day Maggie and I were up early. We were to entertain friends on that day, and on Boxing Day we were to be guests at their home. We had hardly finished breakfast when the first knock came at the door. The caller was Pipes, the morning postman, and he was dressed in his Sunday suit. He was carrying a cardboard carton. 'Merry Christmas,' he said, thrusting the carton at us. 'A special delivery, sort of unofficial.'

The carton was full of envelopes addressed to us, and each envelope contained a card. There were a couple of dozen of them, and not a few small packages. Maggie and I were both touched and embarrassed that so many of the villagers had remembered us. We offered Pipes a drink, and were surprised, it being so early, when he accepted. We had to join him, naturally. We expected him to drink up and then leave, but he settled himself down on a kitchen chair and made himself comfortable. He was still sitting there when the second knock came at the door. The caller this time was Ben, in a suit that we had never seen before, but still wearing his stubble, and smelling overpoweringly of mothballs. He handed Maggie a small gift-wrapped parcel. We had only just poured Ben another drink when there was another knock, and there stood Percy, smart as a new pin, gift in hand. One after another they came, in an endless stream, until Maggie and I had completely lost track of them, and didn't know who we had in the house and who we didn't. We were by this time certain though that any villager who hadn't yet called would certainly do so. And they did. Young 'Enry even brought his wife, who was hardly ever seen in the village, and Whistling Jack looked a stranger in a dark suit instead of the usual blue denims. The older men had each brought some small gift with them, but the younger ones had each brought some type of drink. They each set about drinking as though it was some kind of duty, and Maggie and I had to take some part in it all.

By the time that our expected guests arrived at one thirty, we were both beginning to feel the effects of the many toasts that we had sipped. Miss Money and the vicar's wife had just left, each one supporting the other, and each one certain that the other had had just a little too much. The vicar's wife's speech was a little bit too precise to be natural, and Miss Money's large hat was tipped over at a rakish angle. We were left surrounded by empty glasses and half empty bottles, full ashtrays and half-opened packages. The Christmas dinner hadn't even been started, and our guests were ravenous after their journey. Maggie sorted things out by cooking ham and eggs at once, and we had the Christmas dinner at tea time. By the time that we had eaten that meal we felt sufficiently recovered to join our guests in a toast, but with very little in our two glasses.

When the visitors had left and we were alone, Maggie and I drank one final toast before going to bed. It was with the greatest sincerity that we raised our glasses and said 'A merry Christmas and the very best of New Years to all the people of this village.'

The days, the weeks, the months had flown by, and before we knew it we were approaching the end of January, and we had been at the village Post Office for a whole year. Maggie and I had agreed that we would give the rural life a year's trial, and then decide whether the life really was for us or not. We had been approached by an agent just before Christmas, and knew that we could sell the business at a profit, if that was what we wished to do. We had a decision to make. We knew that we would never get rich, running the village Post Office, but we would make a good living, and in the countryside, where we both now wished to live. The local people had accepted us by now, and we had made a number of very real friends. The social side of the village life could be just as hectic as we wished to make it.

Then we looked round our shop, crowded with stock that we had carefully chosen, and smelling as nothing else in the world except an old-fashioned village store can smell, of sides of bacon and carbolic soap, of pepper and spices and roofing felt. Of ripe red cheese and rubber boots, and any number of other things. The smells combined into one glorious aroma, that brought instant smiles to the faces of any visitors from the city. Then we looked round our comfortable home. The ship in a bottle carefully made for us by Percy. The pictures of wild flowers from Miss Money. The corn dolly, slightly bent, produced by Ben. In the larder a brace of pheasants were hanging, a present from Len. Bundles of dried herbs, bottles of home-made wine, potted plants, Mrs Peckham's beautiful little sampler. Table mats, made by someone just to give to us, shells from summer beaches, enormous horseshoes that we had dug up out of the garden, jars of honey, more than we could ever eat, and apples, polished and stored by crotchety old Charlie.

All these little things had combined together and turned the building into a home, and we knew that we both loved the place. We looked at each other. There was no decision to be made, nothing to talk over. 'The villagers too,' said Maggie, as if she had been reading my thoughts, 'they're like one big family, we couldn't leave them now.'

'Let's go for a walk before supper,' I said, reaching for our coats. 'It's a fine moonlit night, and I hear that a lot of wildfowl have landed on the lake at Lady Blanche's.

We'll probably see one or two of the villagers down there, and you know what they say. If you can't beat 'em . . .' And off we went, to learn just a little more about the Norfolk countryside, and a little more about the Norfolk country people.

THE END

OH, MY DARLING DAUGHTER BY ERIC MALPASS

At seventeen, Viola's dreams of the future hadn't gone much further than marrying the beautiful Reverend Chisholm, the curate from St. Cuthbert's, and having ten children, so taking charge of the family while Mother was off on an eccentric jaunt was rather unexpected. Looking after an eternally grubby little brother, and a sister who knew all about sex and the Thirty Years War but little else, was no easy task – and Father didn't help when he invited the glamorous Gloria to be their 'housekeeper'. The sleepy village of Shepherd's Delight had never seen anything quite like Gloria, and neither had the beautiful Reverend Chisholm! What with that, and the mysterious postcards arriving from Mother in Cairo, Istanbul, Samarkand ... Viola felt that life was getting out of hand ...

0 552 10756 5   80p

A FATHER BEFORE CHRISTMAS BY NEIL BOYD

They're back – the irrepressible Father Charles Duddleswell, the maddening, glorious Mrs. Pring and the innocent Father Neil Boyd – a series of new escapades that will have you rolling in the aisles and, for that matter, in the nave and in the vestry. Funnier and more appealing than ever ...

'An enchanting blend of humour and humanity.' *Sunday Express*

0 552 11010 8   85p

A SELECTION OF FINE TITLES
IN CORGI PRINT

WHILE EVERY EFFORT IS MADE TO KEEP PRICES LOW, IT IS SOMETIMES
NECESSARY TO INCREASE PRICES AT SHORT NOTICE. CORGI BOOKS
RESERVE THE RIGHT TO SHOW AND CHARGE NEW RETAIL PRICES ON
COVERS WHICH MAY DIFFER FROM THOSE ADVERTISED IN THE TEXT
OR ELSEWHERE.

THE PRICES SHOWN BELOW WERE CORRECT AT THE TIME OF GOING
TO PRESS (DEC' 79)

☐	10796 4	The Secret Lemonade Drinker	*Guy Bellamy*	75p
☐	11163 5	Lucia In London	*E. F. Benson*	£1.25
☐	11113 9	Queen Lucia	*E. F. Benson*	95p
☐	10669 0	Bless Me, Father	*Neil Boyd*	75p
☐	11010 8	A Father Before Christmas	*Neil Boyd*	85p
☐	11149 X	Imogen	*Jilly Cooper*	75p
☐	10878 2	Prudence	*Jilly Cooper*	75p
☐	10576 7	Harriet	*Jilly Cooper*	75p
☐	10264 4	The Cedar Tree	*Michael Hardwick*	75p
☐	10818 9	The Cedar Tree: A Bough Breaks	*Michael Hardwick*	80p
☐	10438 8	The Cedar Tree: Autumn Of An Age	*Michael Hardwick*	75p
☐	10755 7	Summer Awakening	*Eric Malpass*	80p
☐	10756 5	Oh, My Darling Daughter	*Eric Malpass*	80p
☐	10626 7	The Long, Long Dances	*Eric Malpass*	75p
☐	10625 9	Morning's At Seven	*Eric Malpass*	70p
☐	98081 1	The Frank Muir Book	*Frank Muir*	£1.95
☐	09891 4	Chia The Wildcat	*Joyce Stranger*	70p
☐	09462 5	Lakeland Vet	*Joyce Stranger*	70p

*All these books are available at your bookshop or newsagent, or can be ordered direct from the pub-
lisher. Just tick the titles you want and fill in the form below.*

CORGI BOOKS. Cash Sales Department, P.O. Box 11, Falmouth, Cornwall.
Please send cheque or postal order, no currency.
U.K. send 22p for first book plus 10p per copy for each additional book ordered to a
maximum charge of 82p to cover the cost of postage and packing.
B.F.P.O. and Eire allow 22p for the first book plus 10p per copy for the next 6 books,
thereafter 4p per book.
Overseas Customers. Please allow 30p for the first book and 10p per copy for each
additional book.

NAME (Block letters) ....

ADDRESS ....

....